LEAD
OR BLEED

The Proven Guide to Building Local Marketing Funnels and Getting Leads

Tom Parsons

HIGH GROUND
BOOKS

Powered by High Ground Books

ATLAS ELITE
PUBLISHING

Published by Atlas Elite Publishing Partners.

Interior design by Michael Beas
Cover design by Jill Parsons

Ebook ISBN: 978-1-962825-81-8
Paperback ISBN: 978-1-962825-82-5
Hardback ISBN: 978-1-962825-83-2

Printed in the United States of America. For more information, visit: www.atlaselitepublishingpartners.com

DEDICATION

I dedicate this book to my wife Alica, who has always believed I'm better than I am; and to my four kids, Thomas, Jill, Juli, and Dane, who have made me the richest man in town.

Your constant belief in me and willingness to listen to my ideas has given me the courage to bring others value no matter the cost.

ENDORSEMENTS

"A rare business book with timeless value. Parsons blends insight and practicality into a guide entrepreneurs and enterprises can use immediately."
Michael Beas
CEO, The Book Revue

"Marketers need practicality when connecting strategy to execution, and *Lead or Bleed* delivers exactly that. Tom gives marketers the framework to advertise smarter and scale faster. This book belongs in the hands of every decision maker in marketing who wants growth that lasts."
Tricia Benn
Partner & Chief Executive Officer, C-Suite Network™,
Podcast & TV Host and Business Disruptor

FOREWORD

By C. Lee Smith

Founder and CEO of SalesFuel, recognized by Selling Power as one of the world's Leading Sales Consultants

You have a business to run. You might even be doing much of the work yourself. Your time is scarce, but you always need money – whether it's to grow or just keep the lights on. Like it or not, marketing is one more necessary challenge on the list.

Tom Parsons reminds us that a brand is more than a logo or slogan—it's a promise. It is your job to communicate that promise and then deliver on it, consistently and memorably. Customers turn to you hoping you'll solve their problem quickly and give them the confidence to act now. If you delight them, they'll return, leave glowing reviews, and send new customers your way — ultimately the most effective marketing you can have.

When it comes to creating, revising and executing your marketing plan, you really have three choices: 1) do it yourself; 2) do it with the help of a trusted advisor; or 3.) hire someone to do it for you.

Today's entrepreneurs and local business owners have unlimited self-service tools at their fingertips. On the surface, it's tempting to go the "do it yourself" route. But what appears easy can quickly turn into a costly money pit. Self-service ad platforms, for example, look simple enough: sign up, pay and launch. Yet beneath that simplicity lies a maze of complexity and risk.

These platforms lead marketers into the ultra-competitive 5% of the market: those already buying and those ready to compare prices and negotiate for even bigger discounts. That approach not only erodes profit but also undermines the meaningful relationships and unique brand differentiation that ensure repeat business.

Making these platforms work well demands expertise and time that most business owners do not have. Add the rise of AI into the mix, and things can become more complicated. AI promises instant copywriting, automated emails, even full campaign launches but too often it delivers average quality work when your company needs A-level results. And when it churns out hallucinations, inaccurate offers or risky claims, whose reputation is on the line? Yours.

Smart business owners use AI for efficiency and brainstorming, but never blindly. Every output needs careful checking, and AI tends to over-recommend digital tactics while neglecting reliable, proven ways to build real value for your brand.

Maybe you can afford a "do it for me" approach, handing marketing off entirely most local business owners do not. If that's your path, remember: oversight is essential. You don't need to know every answer, but you must ask the right questions and keep a close watch on how they spend your money. Otherwise, you risk bleeding cash without results.

And no — giving it to your brother-in-law who posts memes on weekends isn't a viable option. Marketing isn't a hobby project. It's your reputation, your growth, and your bottom line on the line. And let's be real: firing friends and family is even trickier than working with them.

That's where a skilled partner comes in — a specialist who knows your brand, your market, and can untangle your options into a clear, cost-effective plan. The best advisors cut through the noise and make sense of all the options available. They help you tackle your biggest challenges to generating revenue — simply, consistently and affordably.

And they keep you on track, never forgetting to put your customer in the spotlight. These are the people who turn to you hoping you'll solve their problem quickly and give them the confidence to act now. The customers you serve are your reason for being in business.

"Lead or Bleed" is not an invitation to go it alone. It's a roadmap for becoming a better, smarter client who can collaborate with agencies, marketing advisors and media reps to achieve the best results for your business. This book arms you with that mindset, empowering you to steer your marketing partners in the right direction for real business impact. After all, no one knows your business better.

Based on Tom's decades as a sought-after marketing advisor, this book will guide you through the choices, the pitfalls, and the partnerships that matter. You'll build an excellent BS detector and lead the conversation about how to talk to your customers. It's about making smart decisions with marketing — so your brand promise stands out, your leads grow, and your business doesn't just survive — it thrives.

About C. Lee Smith

C. Lee Smith is a global authority on business credibility and leadership. Named by *Selling Power* as one of the world's top sales consultants, he helps executives strengthen influence, leverage AI, and build trust with clients.

As founder and CEO of **SalesFuel®**, Lee created **AdMall®**, the leading sales intelligence platform empowering local media and agencies to help small businesses grow. A Certified Behavioral Analyst, he blends market and behavioral insights to improve marketing, messaging, and management decisions.

Lee is the Amazon international bestselling author of *SalesCred* and *The Leader's Playbook*, a contributor to *Entrepreneur*, and co-host of the *Manage Smarter* podcast — ranked among the world's top business management shows. Learn more at **cleesmith.com**.

TABLE OF CONTENTS

Introduction... 1

Chapter 1: Make Your Vows 5

Chapter 2: Two Roads Diverged 9

Chapter 3: Grit Over Gravity 17

Chapte r 4: From Chaos to Constant 22

Chapter 5: We Want It Now.. 28

Chapter 6: How Did We Get Here? 32

Chapter 7: Over- Indexing On One Format 41

Chapter 8: Familiarity Seeds Intent 48

Chapter 9: Verify First Vs. Trust First...................... 78

Chapter 10: The Tush Push Of Intent 103

Chapter 11: The Lit Match of Loyalty....................... 124

Chapter 12: The Balancing Act 141

Chapter 13: Before You Buy 156

Chapter 14: After You Buy Ads 163

Chapter 15: The Brad Pitt Of Marketing.................. 170

Chapter 16: Stealing Torture 175

Chapter 17: Using AI to Your Advantage................. 183

Chapter 18: About Your Sales Reps 195

Chapter 19: How to Buy Streaming Television Ads 203

Conclusion 211

INTRODUCTION

L et me start by identifying the elephant in the room. If you offer a product or service that delights customers better than the competition, you don't need ANY of what I'm about to tell you.

"Hey Tom, ummm ... that's not a good way to start a book about marketing," you might say.

And you'd be right, IF the company you lead marketing has the best marketing channel of all time, positive word of mouth. If your company delivers an experience that is unlike any other in the field, and is known to delight customers at every level, it's true that you need little to no marketing and advertising. The vehicle that is positive word of mouth is so swift, so powerful, and so viral, you won't need it. I have made a quarter-century career, however, on the fact negative word of mouth works even faster.

As I have spoken with literally thousands of companies, the overwhelming majority of which are NOT delighting all customers at every level, it's extremely important that I get this concept out of the way. Those with insanely good customer experiences can put this book back and choose a title like *Raving Fans* by Ken Blanchard or Delivering Happiness by the late Tony Hsieh to confirm they are on the right path.

So I turn to those who can be honest about what they can or can't do in their role. What about those who don't have companies like this? What about those who are only responsible and accountable for the marketing in a company whose attention to service is led by someone else whom they don't influence? What if the kind of company you are doesn't have a clear path to becoming the best at delighting customers until you get some?

I'd like to introduce you to three hypothetical people in three different real local-market scenarios who DON'T have the greatest value of positive word of mouth working for them, at least not yet ...

Riley is a first-time marketing director of a local bank. Her experience in college was working as a social media coordinator for an event marketing company who now has the responsibility of planning media and messaging to meet the bank's advertising and sponsorship objectives. She's just learned their large budget is half of what it once was but growth targets appear to mirror last year's goals. The previous director left due to this. Riley needs to make this first big opportunity of her career to work.

Chris most recently did marketing for a software company that sold data solutions to other businesses. His brother owns a two-location furniture store in town and has convinced Chris to come take care of his advertising and marketing and scale the business together. Chris is smart but the local marketing ecosystem that serves consumers is very different from what he knows best. Family dynamics are going to shift considerably if Chris doesn't get it right.

Vanessa runs a four-person marketing team in a $25 million HVAC business. She reports to a CEO with much bigger goals and expects every dollar to have a specified justification and set of metrics in order to be spent. To beat the largest players in the marketplace, some great things must need to take place but the budget remains flat. The pressure on Vanessa to deliver is strong.

As if each of these hopeful marketers aren't staring at a mountain to climb, they have dozens of local media vendors calling on them every week. All of them claim the "best thing" on the market in some way. Making matters worse, marketing headlines that should help them figure out how to climb the mountain seem to contradict each other regularly. It's a mess for marketers to deal with.

Do any of these strike a nerve with you? Based on the stories I hear, it most likely does, and it leaves you wondering what to do next. How does someone with limited resources maximize leads, know what's working, and keep from bleeding cash?

That's what this book is about.

Too many local marketers share too many of the same pain points. Someone needs to show you what's behind the curtain.

Someone needs to reveal to you what successful companies are doing and how to imitate the strategies and the results relative to size. This is what I want to do for you.

I will have been successful by the end of this book if:

1. You have a clear understanding of what your business's promise is to the market.
2. You know what it takes to deliver on that promise every day.
3. You build belief in that promise in your future customers.
4. You know what is available to you in your local market.
5. You have a full custom marketing funnel built from what is available to you locally.
6. You know how to adapt to what the data tells you and repeat only better.
7. You have fun running your marketing plan.

It's a tall order, but I accept the challenge. I don't want the value that I can offer you to be wasted by not sharing what I know. If I can make you better in these areas, it will be worth it. YOU are worth it. So, let's do this!

Fair warning: I use a lot of analogies, and one of my dangerous pastimes is mixing metaphors. I'll check in on you now and again, but I want to make sure I connect you with value by way of stories and word pictures. That is how I am built, so proceed cautiously. Apologies to Dr. Chapman, my Advanced Grammar and Composition 401 professor. I did my best, sir. Thanks for passing me.

Chapter 1

MAKE YOUR VOWS

What is Your Brand?

Before we talk about delivery methods and strategies that work for you, we have to make sure what's in the delivery vehicle is worth taking to your future customers. You may have a unique product or service, but many of you have similar offers being delivered. That fact makes marketing difficult, because you'll look and sound like everyone else. You will either have to make a unique offer and message or be willing to outspend the competition to keep a share of people's attention.

And while attention is primary, it's not exclusive. You have to promise something so that people follow attention with action. Don't worry, this chapter is going to help make that easier, because I'm sure you are more like the characters in my introduction, who all have budget pressures but may not realize you have a unique promise that you can keep. And that's what brands are about.

If you ask 100 people what a brand is, you'll get 112 different answers. Very few people understand what a brand really is. Some of the answers will be the colors, logo, font ... concrete visuals that are easy to recognize. Others will say it's the vibe of a business ... the energy it gives off. Each of these answers and many like it dance around what a brand is but don't cut straight to the core of it. A brand is a promise that you can keep, and it has to be something people care about.

Know Who You Are

Take a very close look at what you deliver. What is the highest guarantee or promise you can make? Your marketing will expose and amplify the realities of too-small promises you can keep or too-big promises you can't keep. So before advertising any of these promises, make sure you are prepared to articulate what you deliver well and deliver it consistently. It will save you a ton of money on advertising by way of better voice; it will help you make easier message delivery decisions; and it will make plenty of room for creativity.

Role Play:

I mentioned Riley in the introduction. She's just been given marketing responsibilities at the local bank. They've always advertised their competitive rates and their long history in the community. But for Riley, if she is looking at making a promise that customers care about, she'll have to overcome the lack of convenience to the entire community, both geographically and technologically. What does she do? She has to look at what else might matter to their customers; which upon deeper inspection, it's obvious there's something they do that others don't. They make local decisions because they serve their neighbors. The bank's customers are probably going to know the loan officers from the little league field, church, or the chamber of commerce. Immediately, Riley has a better promise to offer the community, and it didn't change anything about how the bank does business.

The bank's promise is that the people making decisions about your loans are local. You aren't just an account number with us. You're our neighbor, and that familiarity is special for you. We'll get to Riley's delivery methods later, but from the outset, any marketing materials she produces and any advertising she does will be easier because Riley knows the unique promise her bank delivers and what difference that makes to her audience.

And here, we park at an important truth, taught to me by one of my advertising heroes, Roy H. Williams, the Wizard of Ads. The truth? When it comes to messaging, "the risk of insult is the price of clarity." Clarity plants a seed in good ground and doesn't worry about other ground where ideas can grow. The leadership team is going to question Riley's decision to get out of the rate discussion and the misplaced storytelling about how long the bank has been in business. And the friction could derail her because to them, she is leaving out the part of the market that clearly buys on rates. The proven reality is that you will get those too, but the scarcer Riley's resources, the narrower her focus has to be.

People opt in to the crystal-clear clarity of your offer because you have delivered a promise that all people care about and who they care about - themselves. And a cool feature in this case is that Riley can still convey the trusted years in business as a bank without having to take over the hero spot in the customer's story. This bank is the local guide people can count on, and with this seed, Riley will dominate this belief in the market. Over and over, brands that are specific about who they are and what they are to whom will also acquire business from those who are not in their segment. Remember this for later when we talk about targeted advertising, because it is critical for those decisions.

Think it Through

As you will see woven through every element of this guidebook, the messaging matters more than people think, and that is your first major advantage. Here are some checkpoints to ensure that if you have answers, you are ready for the next chapters:

* In your weakest area, what is the highest guarantee you can make?

* Everyone has customers A to Z, but who do you attract most?

* Is the customer you attract, the customer you want?

* What problem do you help them solve?

Chapter 2

TWO ROADS DIVERGED

What makes them say yes to you?

We just discussed understanding who you are and who you want to be to the world, and the next critical step is examining *why your customer buys from you.* If you haven't fully established that as a business yet, examine why you want them to buy so we have a mutual place to start.

There are two main motivations for people when they are in the market for a product or service. The first is a relational motivation, and the second is a transactional motivation. Let me develop each clearly.

Relational Buyers

One day, you are driving home from work, and a loud clanking sound is coming from the engine, and the service engine soon light comes on. Not this again! If you are like me, you can open up the hood and look at it like you might be able to tell what's going on, but you certainly aren't going to know how to fix it yourself. You're going to need to take it in for service. Where do you take it?

Each of us has a place like that we always take our vehicles for service. For those of us who have been through enough car issues, we know exactly where we will go next with it without any hesitation.

How did we make that leap so fast? Why didn't we go to our TVs and start watching for an ad to pop up? Why didn't we start scrolling Facebook to see if we could get a service station ad? And why didn't we go to Google and type in a generic search and see what pops up? Of the three, that seems most logical, but we don't do that. Why?

The simple truth is that once we have someplace we trust, we just go there.

What about the pricing? Didn't a direct competitor to the place you take it just send you a direct mail piece with a special offer for the very service you know your vehicle needs? Why didn't you take that in to redeem the special great deal? You know where I'm going with this. Trust is a hard thing to overcome, which is why so many companies still put a great amount of their advertising into growth marketing when push comes to shove. It's hard to topple a trusted competitor, but once you are there, it's also hard to topple you. If you have a product or service that requires high trust, your job is to recruit a relational buyer with your advertising message and media types, and you'll find that price isn't a leading factor for them.

There are probably cheaper service stations, but you probably take your car to the same place every single time. They have your car's history. They know you when you walk in. They treat you like you're a regular. Perhaps they know that making a promise of good service and they keep that promise. That's enough.

As far as you know, their pricing is competitive. However, the effect of that simple truth is that "switching costs" are real to you, even if they are imagined. You don't want to mess around with price shopping. You want experts who will get it done right, done quickly, and not look for ways to make you pay more for stuff you don't need.

Do you see the thought processes of a relational buyer here? As the buyer, you have a certain approach:

- Long time horizon on the purchase
- Affinity as a main driver of choices
- Value-driven decisions
- Need expertise from the advertiser

Transactional Buyers

It sounds nice to talk about value, loyalty, and trust. But that's not the only reason people buy things. They also buy on price. And if your business indeed has the most effective pricing model in the market, you're going to win a lot here. The transactional buyers will flock to this kind of business, at least temporarily.

Let's continue with the automotive theme. My main contact at my favorite automotive repair shop is Rick. He tells me it might be time to pull the trigger on getting a new car, because mine is 13 years old, and the issues are not only expensive to fix, they are indicative that I'm going to keep having to pump thousands of dollars into it again soon, possibly indefinitely.

So I'm suddenly in the market for a car. What do I do?

As with many of you, it's a combination of many places I would look, but if I'm going new, I'm probably going to head online to an aggregator for the next few days while also paying closer attention to the ads on all kinds of media that come my way.

The landscape on cars has changed since the last one I bought 13 years ago, so I'm starting fresh. When the critical timing comes, I've narrowed it down to a make and model I want, now it's down to who has that exact car and color I prefer.

Scrolling down the list after putting in my filters, I find a dealership that has what I want for $800 cheaper than everyone else. Of course, I'm calling them and giving them the chance to close me on that car.

The simple truth in this case is that if price is my leading consideration, the lowest price wins.

What about loyalty? Service after the sale? Convenience for warranty work? For transactional buyers, these might be on the list, but there's a wide distance between those things and price, as it stands atop the priority list for this type of consumer.

And for many years, the automotive industry has spent the most on advertising, recruiting this type of customer with their ads. A spokesman swinging his arms, shouting prices and terms of the deal, and lots of flashing lights and colors have all been part of the advertising ecosystem for dealers because they believe the buyer wants the best price more than they want anything else. And for decades, we have convinced them that this is true by our behavior. Our actions don't lie. Let's summarize the decision processes of the transactional buyer here:

- Shorter time horizon on the purchase.
- Comparison shopping from the customer.
- Price-driven decisions.
- Done their own homework as their own expert.

Role Play:

Remember Chris from our introduction? After walking through all that his brother has been trying to execute in marketing the furniture store, he recognized immediately that the company has been competing on price the entire time. The problem is that they aren't winning on price enough. The big box stores have more competitive pricing and their operational efficiencies are helping keep it that way.

The one advantage Chris appears to have is an exclusive deal for a high-end furniture brand as the only provider of those luxury pieces in town. But since they are only recruiting the transactional buyer who knows what they are looking for and can see online at their store or the giant chain what the price is, store traffic is really low. The intrusive visibility and convenience of the two locations have kept them relevant for now, along with the great margins of the exclusive luxury brand deal.

Chris knows that if they are going to gain share in the market, they are going to have to decide who they want. Do they keep fighting for the transactional buyer and perhaps take a bigger hit to margins by getting more competitive with price, and try to make it up with volume? Or do they stop fighting what looks like a losing battle and use the advantage they have and expand their reach to the upscale clientele?

For that, I turn to Sun Tzu's *The Art of War*. To fight the competition, you can win easily when holding positions that cannot be attacked because they are left behind or unavailable to the enemy.

As long as Chris can market this exclusive relationship, he can march into the market where the enemy is not without a counterattack. This furniture store can become the first name in luxury living if he can convince his brother to expand this offer and sell off what's left of the commoditized items to people who perhaps want the luxury but can't afford it.

Additionally, as we'll discuss in later chapters, the brand's messaging again is critical, and the advertising channels must convey the exclusivity of the opportunity. And finally, the price-conscious consumer must be ignored for the "good ground" Chris will plant the seeds of growth. Ignoring a segment of the market may sound harsh, but there is great news. Those people will not feel ignored. In fact, they will feel called up.

When Red Bull launched its energy boosting drink to Americans needing an energy pick-me-up in 1997, they were very specific about who their target was and why they would buy.

But wouldn't you know it, adrenaline thrill seekers weren't the only fans chugging it, despite to this day tying together with extreme sports as its focus. How did Red Bull also pull in professionals, night owls, and soccer moms? They didn't worry about speaking to anyone but adrenaline junkies. And that's another secret you now have in your arsenal. Drawing that line makes people to want to cross it. Making the other side of the line exciting or attractive makes them hurry across.

Think it Through

* Why do they buy from you? Is it more logical or emotional?

* What emotional or logical response do you want from your target? Is it different than what you are getting?

* Why will your fans love you?

Chapter 3

GRIT OVER GRAVITY

It's a Climb Upward, Not a Chute Downward

O nce you have a message that matters to people, it's time to get it out. The untrained marketer will just choose a few trusted reps in the market for mass media and try to save some money in-house if they have the headcount with everything else. Some might not be able to keep it in-house and will hire a so-called digital agency that will handle their digital footprint and possibly some digital advertising.

"The weaker they are as thinkers, the more due diligence they do."
-Charlie Munger

At the same time, the marketer on the other end of this idea might veer into putting the message only in places where the exact attribution can be made to that ad, which typically tends to be what many refer to as digital products. Vanessa at the HVAC company in the introduction definitely has a CEO who tends to think this way, and both of these marketing styles are riddled with problems.

The problem starts when a marketer thinks of advertising as either traditional or digital, also defined by some as growth marketing vs. performance marketing. No matter how you see the terms, thinking of marketing funnels this way only is going to cause you trouble based on the types of customers I spoke of in the last chapter. Messaging might fit well into these two types, but the delivery vehicles don't function that way, and this will box you in.

In order to make a great marketing funnel, we first need to understand that it is a climb that closes customers at the summit of the mountain. Typical marketing funnel visuals make the customer journey look like it's a children's board game, where you start with traditional/growth media and your leads will pick up steam with digital media, nice and easy, where the metrics are clear and assignable to the digital ad, and the ROI is immediately clear.

But this isn't how it works in your future customers' minds, and the difficulty in getting them to come to you instead of someone else gets harder, not easier. That sounds more like a mountain trail hike to the top rather than a Chutes C Ladders game. The good news is that I am going to equip you with the tools for you to make the customer's climb much easier, and perhaps even bypass a lot of the treachery that mountain hiking can offer them.

The Segments of the Customer Journey

In addition to the widely accepted marketing funnel being more difficult and treacherous than the visuals convince you they are, there are a lot of marketing entities that assign names to the parts of the customer journey. And they aren't wrong necessarily. It's just that the more you get into this, the more you realize a simpler format is necessary in a local market. More parts pop up for various reasons too, so it's just too complicated for a local plumber who just wants to do more plumbing work. Currently, there are more than a dozen funnel frameworks out there that are accepted in the industry. And like I said, they aren't all wrong. Just too complicated. So let me simplify it for you.

For this book, let's say there are only three pre-sale segments of the customer journey, and one post-sale that we'll discuss in detail later. Right now, I want to focus on the three core segments: Awareness, Consideration, and Intent. They may sound self-explanatory, which is part of why I reduced it to these, but there is also an additional method in it. And here I need to pause to tell you that this is a great intersection of math, science, philosophy and art, where the rule of thirds makes it so much easier to digest complex concepts.

The Easiest Polygon to Draw

Since we are calling it a mountain hike upward and not a slide downward, imagine a triangle, much like you see in a traditional marketing funnel, only upside down to look more like a mountain.

The bottom of the funnel is the wide opening, which we'll call **Awareness**; the middle of the funnel is **Consideration,** and the tip at the top is **Intent.** No surprises there besides inverting it, but in this funnel are funnels within each, and all three segments have three segments as their own funnel inside them. Call it a variation on the Sierpinski Triangle for those of you who are also really into math, but each funnel has its own Awareness, Consideration, and Intent inside it.

Once you realize this, you can make quick leaps forward in thinking about how to build a lead program through your marketing and advertising channels.

And the good news is that in each stage of the funnel, you can more distinctly predict what intent is for that segment. As you will see, the action to be taken in each part of the funnel is likely different and more intense.

Your job in this view is to determine which media fills your funnels well enough to keep the pipeline moving. *It's a difficult journey to the top, but the leads, by volume and value, will increase with dramatic effect over time.* The rest of this book is to help you determine what the right fit is for your business based on many factors. See the questions below and get a firm grasp of these, because it will also be part of your decision-making process.

Think it Through

* How long a process does someone take to make their decision about buying your product or service and the industry as a whole when it's not an emergency situation?

* How does the average sale or price point for your industry compare to other industries?

* What percentage of your business depends on repeating business with the same customer?

* How seasonal is your industry? Are there times of year there are no sales?

Chapter 4

FROM CHAOS TO CONSTANT

The Day the World Changed Forever

Where were you on Monday, January 3rd, 1983? Many changes came to world history that day, but there was one much more "game-changing" than the rest. Sports fans might recall that Tony Dorsett of the Cowboys set an NFL record that evening on Monday Night Football for the longest run from scrimmage against the Vikings, 99 yards. That's amazing because that record has only been or ever will be tied, never broken.

If you are a business history fan, you might easily recognize this date as the day Steve Jobs and Steve Wozniak incorporated Apple Computers. That might be a better idea of noting the world changed forever, but certainly, it can't be as notable as the fact that on this day, the network protocols were officially converted into the global internet we recognize today. The modern internet was born, and yet, there was still something much bigger that happened.

I'm referring to the literal game changer. In the middle of that Monday morning, television audiences all over the U.S. saw Bob Barker introduce a brand-new game of chance that is still the most popular game in Price Is Right history. That world-changing game, of course, is Plinko.

We've all seen it played on days we stayed home from school because we were ill. With our soda and crackers at our side, we'd watch a contestant, by guessing well at prices of household goods, to earn chips to drop down the Plinko board toward a variety of cash values. What made the game more unpredictable is that there were pegs stretched across the board all the way down. Chip placement against the board as gravity took its course couldn't assure the contestant that they'd land at one of the higher cash values or at least avoid the zero-dollar values.

Complex Lives

The game changer for you in this story is a critical one for understanding your customers. And before I pick on them a bit, remember that you and I are customers of someone else's too, and we are not immune to the Plinko effect of advertising and marketing either. The world we live in is a chaotic mess, and before I help you with crucial strategies, it's important to at least recognize why so much diligence is in order.

Advertisers used to be able to sponsor a show like "I Love Lucy" and half the country would see it and would buy the product as advertised. There were very few local options outside a couple of editions of the newspaper and some other local print, a small variety of radio stations, and three local news providers. It was much easier to build trust than it once was.

Additionally, people weren't scheduled and committed back then like they are today. In many ways, it was much simpler. We could talk for hours about the causes of this, both external and internal forces, but our modern reality reveals that we are stretched in many ways, and for you, trying to have a warm, trust-building message feels like it's too wide a chasm to bridge. Everyone is shouting over each other on hundreds of daily media options to consume. It can make your future customer feel like a giant Plinko chip careening through life, just trying to get to the next right thing. Life's distractions and competing priorities bounce them around and make them cynical at least or apathetic at most.

Information Overload

For years, various groups have tried to quantify how many times a day people are presented with an ad. Forbes and the American Marketing Association agree that it's generally 4,000-10,000 times A DAY. Every time I ask this question in a keynote speech, the audience drastically underestimates the number and you probably would too. We just don't think it's happening to us that often, and the reasons a varied and extensive. Here are three main ones:

1. We ignore most of it because it is irrelevant at that moment.

Trying to catch a prospect at the exact right time, especially the broader the media reach, is nearly impossible to predict. I once had a personal injury attorney ask me point-blank if the video data we had access to could predict when someone was going to be in a vehicular accident. Think about that for a minute. You can get pretty good at being in the right place by looking up where accidents occur most in town, but the right time? "If I could do that," I told her, "we'd be having this meeting in our office instead of yours."

While some timing and relevance can be predicted, the majority of advertisers can't know exactly when someone is going to act. For example, a florist can well predict that men will be in the market a few weeks ahead of Valentine's Day, and Mother's Day flowers are a pretty good bet for timing ads when the wallet is open. But what about assisted living? How does an advertiser know when the right time is to market to the family of a loved one? The answer is that they don't, so that kind of advertiser must recognize there will be some waste unless they get the ones who show signs in their behavior. Until then, unless their messaging is seed planting based, they might just be noise to the future customer who doesn't know they will be in the market soon.

2. We ignore even more of it, even if it is relevant, when the messaging sounds like everyone else.

As I promised earlier in this book, the power of the message done well overcomes so much. The cynicism, the apathy, the potential to annoy…all of them slip away when an advertiser goes back to that unique promise that a customer cares about and then keeps it when they call, click, or visit. I can't stress enough and will stress again later how incredibly important it is that you have something that people care about that they will want to opt into. Your business depends on it more than the rest of the data and strategies.

3. We DON'T ignore it, but our minds don't actively think to categorize it.

Let's say you attend a summer event in the park and among other sponsors, Riley and her bank team members are passing out ice-cold drinks, and all you saw was the logo on a polo shirt she was wearing. You are thankful for the refreshment, but you don't really think to associate this with the bank. But three months later, you have a positive feeling without being able to associate the memory when someone tells you they got an auto loan at Riley's bank. Even now, you think that is one ad. Technically, it's two. Your friend using word of mouth under the guise of idle chatter is a second impression Riley didn't pay to be part of.

This happens day after day in thousands of unexpected, unpredictable, and unassuming ways, and unless you have one of those highly superior autobiographical memories (HSAM), you lose it for a time or forever because the seed wasn't planted deep enough, or it wasn't watered, or it got no sunlight. Sometimes it's a combination of all of those, until one or more of the other factors appear, and immediately there can be a spark of growth in the mind and possibly the heart of the potential customer to Riley's community bank in this case.

So far, this book has been difficult news to process, but I appreciate you staying this far. I promise I'm going to make it more fun. But until then, there's another issue that every advertiser must deal with so I have one last pill for you to take before we get really deep in the "how-tos." The issue has to do with who is and ISN'T in the market.

Think it Through

* What ways do you think your message resonates to a stretched and distracted society?

* What ways can your product or service give peace to a prospect in such an environment described here?

* What ways can your business produce additional conversation you didn't have to pay for?

Chapter 5

WE WANT IT NOW

The Impatience of Our Time

One of the reasons the end of the consumer purchase funnel is so competitive is because of what the internet has done for the convenience of finding information during the 21st century. We live in the information age, where anything we want to know is just a click or two away. And a quarter of the way through the century, we have gotten even more impatient. That's not what this chapter is about, but stay with me, because the context of it is extremely important.

When Google perfected the search engine, everyone loved the idea of asking it a question and getting a curated list of possible options or answers, aggregated based on Google's proprietary algorithm. This set of rules became extremely good at validating and ranking options based on many factors, and it worked, year after year. The phone book thinned out and grabbed an online rope to keep from drowning, but it was too late to win. Google had delighted searchers of information too well, and advertisers basked in the sunlight of getting access to the part of the market that wants their goods and services in the timing an advertiser could better predict than ever.

It's obvious that people will still use search engines for aggregated information, and we're going to talk about this extensively in a later chapter, but several events during the 2020s has changed the game again. Current antitrust lawsuits are lodged against Google, starting with but not limited to the DOJ's belief that Google unlawfully maintains search dominance because they pay to be the default search engine on some devices. That may be true, but when online searchers open Bing or Yahoo as the default on their device and still type Google into the search box to go there to search, one could argue that Google is the default in peoples' brains because of how good and valid it is, not just because they are the paid default on peoples' devices.

Additionally, and more relevant to this book, the rise of Artificial Intelligence (AI) like Chat GPT and Copilot has revealed that in many cases, people are so impatient, they don't want a list of valid options as much anymore. They just want the technology to just give them the answer. Google has worked feverishly to compete by providing Gemini, which gives a singular answer with other options below it. Like I said earlier, we're going to discuss the effects of this later, but that is changing the game for advertisers who want to get top billing on the first page of the Search Engine Results Page (SERP).

All that set as our backdrop, understand that this evolution of offering value to searchers and validity to advertisers has made every company take note and put significant effort into the part of the market that is IN the market right now, which research suggests is only 5% of the market on average.

95/5 Rule

The 95/5 rule is a marketing principle we must develop understanding about before we work on building your funnel. Many of you are going to have a hard time fighting the urge to just load up only when the customer's wallet is open. But this is the problem with 21st-century online advertising options. It forces advertisers into a comparison-shopping offer and removes the love affair that advertisers once had with its customers.

Companies that can only separate themselves by price comparisons in the copy of their listings are stripped of the nuance that make for good choices.

By allowing yourself to broaden your thought processes on the 95% of the market who are still at the top or bouncing around somewhere on that Plinko board of life, you earn the opportunity to own relationships that are largely rented in the 5%. So much of the power of media to start a quiet conversation and create interest and even attraction is outside the media options that cater well to that 5%.

If you think I'm suggesting you can ignore that last 5%, you are mistaken. It's important, but the rest of this book is going to help you see what is in the 95%, what's in the 5%, and how much to devote to each. It will never be an either/or recommendation. It will be a proper balance conversation.

The factors are varied, but you will know which are your constants, so you can make a great plan. And even better, I'm going to show you how to make more out of the 5% than your competitors do, and not have to use price as your way to seal the deal with future customers.

Think it Through

* What ways do you differentiate yourself in the market when speaking to the prospect that is definitely ready to buy but is comparison shopping? Is it price? Or perhaps value add for the same price?

* Can you thrive on the comparison shopper? Or does it feel like just surviving?

* What might have to change in your messaging and strategy to pursue a "love affair" with the 95% of the market not yet ready to buy from you?

Chapter 6

HOW DID WE GET HERE?

Single, Looking to Mingle

Imagine you are single. But not just any kind of single. Imagine being the kind of single that is young and full of possibilities. Not so young that you are naïve to the world and the dangers that lurk, but young enough that playing "hard-to-get" is a useful strategy. You certainly aren't playing "beat the clock," like some character in a popular trope in Hollywood films, where the protagonist has until a certain time and date they must be officially married to the love of their life before losing out on some great fortune.

No, you're single, looking for a long-term connection, but you are willing to wait for the right one because you can. You don't have to settle down yet, but you won't keep yourself on the dating scene if you find someone you match well with that mutually meets all the criteria you both would have for a partner. Suffice it to say you have plenty of time and room in your heart to be patient and observant of people you might want to spend the rest of your life with.

But where do you start? Do you even "start?" Do you just live your life being available and let it come to you? If you don't want to just be visible and present, where do you go to find someone that best fits your lifestyle and values right up front? Many Americans who are on a perceived or real time crunch or don't like the hassle of real-world issues will make their start online and work their way backward into relationship with others.

I saw an infographic recently showing the change in American culture for how people have found their spouses. Introductions were made by family, friends, and co-workers mostly and the places were at school, work, church, or other physical social settings not designed for dating necessarily. As the graphics moved through decades, shifts in this dynamic changed rapidly. When dating apps took off in their early years, the number who found their person online went from zero to nearly a third of all new marriages. As of 2024, around 60% of newlywed couples met online, through a dating site, social media, or other internet venue. What a paradigm shift!

"Hey Tom," you're probably thinking, "I thought you were going to talk about helping me build my funnel. What gives?" My answer is, did you think I wasn't? I most certainly was. I can't think of a better example of what has happened to the marketing funnel via advertising in the 21st century than the timing similarities of online dating.

Traditional Values

Let me pause here. If you think I'm down on online dating and by proxy online advertising, I most assuredly am not. I love people who met each other online, and I am so glad they did. There is a place for this in society. I also like some of the effects online advertising can have on triggering action. But I want to highlight the similarities to show how we can incorporate the online relationships, social or economic, personal or business, rather than having it take over real-life connections.

Before Google figured out how to be better than any other search engine back in the late 90's, a local advertiser seemingly had it made. They could start a relationship with their customer in many formats, all with seed-planting, belief-driven, emotion-led advertising. Grab the entire geographic market area with broadcast TV, tighten the targets a bit and get on a few local cable networks, blow up top-of-mind with terrestrial radio, provide a special deal or two in the paper for conversion, and make sure you can be found in the phone book with a basic or even larger, more colorful listing once a year.

Bigger advertisers who wanted to dominate their local region would buy TV time from multiple broadcasters and perhaps sponsor a local news segment; add fixed programming in cable news, sports, and entertainment; multiply frequency with extra radio formats; take out a double truck ad in the newspaper with something truly remarkable; and make unique offers on whole pages of the phone book or even buy the back cover. Perhaps to go even further, they'd go from sponsoring some little league teams to purchasing naming rights on a local venue.

Then Came Tech

Advertising was fun for them. Run the simple formula, watch the sales numbers grow. Nobody had to individually prove their worth outside of the whole marketing plan. If their service was good, if their product was distinctive, and if everyone could see and hear what was out there by and large, they'd judge the effect with their personal polls themselves along with the sales numbers. Word of mouth was much easier to gauge. People trusted what they saw without a lot of cynicism.

As the internet grew and normalized itself after the dot-com bubble burst, options exploded. Websites started monetizing online billboards and offering impressions for sale based on information they could pull from known users. Publishers first started selling them directly to advertisers, but that got too complicated, so exchanges were born. People could buy what was now called display ads on an electronic exchange, similar to the way stocks are traded, but in milliseconds in a real-time bidding process.

At the same time, Google and the remaining search engines used the same bid process for businesses as people flocked to get information in search engine results pages. While large agencies and publishers built exchanges for buying and selling online ad units of rapidly expanding options, big tech giants created their own walled gardens to have the buying and selling done from their own platforms because they could. Google, Amazon, Meta, Apple, and TikTok all have self-serve ad platforms that can't be bought from outside those gardens.

Don't get me wrong, while dating apps helping people find the love of their lives is really cool, it altered our social system in a way that has also produced some negative results. What started as a way to help people find their permanent match has potentially led to sub-optimal situations. People may be using them for hook-up culture or worse, and the same can be said proverbially for advertisers of all varieties. Some advertisers care more about their profits than the customer, for instance. The seller side has a long history of fraud and people have been sold a bill of goods that has gotten them zero results.

Meanwhile, good-hearted, growth-driven businesses that just want to create a long-term connection with customers in a mutually beneficial relationship have two choices. They can stick with being the right one and stay present in the traditional spaces where a good match can find them for when the timing is right; or, they can get in line with the dating apps for advertising.

Swipe Right

We'll talk more about this in the chapter on intent media, but for now, to understand the ecosystem of the funnel you will build, you have to recognize that advertisers have shifted a ton of their advertising to online environments where the action is trackable.

Click attribution is the "swipe right" of customer dating, and the fact that so many marriages have resulted, it can make an advertiser think it has to be there, too. The data supports this on many levels.

However, businesses stopped the courtship process in the last two decades in favor of getting data upfront and swiping on customers who are in the market right now. Sinking into the particulars of meeting new customers from a deeper level for later has been replaced with electronic speed dating that gets to the bottom line right now. Couple this information with what I told you earlier about the 95% of the market not really interested or available right now for many reasons, the fight for a match is fierce, and it stays ultra-competitive for the duration of the search for customers. This is has worn out a lot of earnest advertisers, and they can't immediately detect why.

Like worthy young people still looking for a permanent partner, they keep recruiting people who just want a date for Friday night. There's some temporary fun in that, but it doesn't solve the nagging problem that they can't live like this forever if they want to create a legacy with customers for life. Now, with this tension between Awareness and Intent, enter Consideration stage left, and cue some relief.

Bridge the Great Divide

There is a massive distance between the concept of wooing customers for when the time is right by being present but not desperate and the concept of needing to hook up now with a special offer. There has to be something that helps a company move between these two types of situations toward a permanent relationship without losing margins or not getting sales at all. Consideration Media has filled that void. As a stage of the journey, it largely did not exist to bridge the gap between the foundation and peak of the funnel for most of the 20th century. With cynicism being low, and lack of other options being available, most of what is used to bridge the gap in advertising in the funnel wasn't necessary either. TV and other mass media outlets could just stay present with a gondola ride of sorts from the base of the mountain to the peak where the sale is, and the customers would step out with their cash when it was time to do so.

But as more trust in advertising was broken, people put their cash-filled hands back in their pockets and they started asking more questions. They started listening more to what people said about where they made their purchases that we might need to make soon, and they went on the hunt for more data to prove why they should buy from this company they've heard about. As the quest for more proof became necessary, the internet provided more capability to take slower steps, make the climb, and be more accomplished in their decision-making.

The trap many advertisers who were smaller previously fall into is that they don't make the tough leap back to the base of the funnel at awareness, then cross the bridge of consideration. They try to use consideration media to keep the intent level messaging. This will make them fail because they still look like they are in temporary relationship mode.

The medium and the message need to balance both long-term and short-term relationship status vibes at this stage. More powerful value to come on that last sentence, but understand this powerful truth about the psychology of this funnel when starting at the end and working your way backward to awareness instead of the other way around:

Too much intent in your consideration phase and you look like a stalker at worst and at best still a "pick me." Both are a turn-off for customers who want brands they trust but also fair pricing. Think about it. There's a brand you don't know using text ads on your phone, offering you a discount on a product or service you aren't in the market for and don't have any idea what the best price would be for that. Immediate turn off. This kind of thing is happening way more than it should.

Understand the phases of the ecosystem, value the journey customers are on, and know how your product or service fits into and messages correctly to them, and the three chapters on each phase's main ad products are going to be a walk in the park for you to comprehend. We're going to take a quick exit to fuel up for that journey in the next chapter, but we're going to make this business fun again.

Think it Through

* Without going too deep into the analogy, does the similarities of the advertising ecosystem and the world of online dating for marriage resonate with you? How can you use this when making messaging and ad buying decisions?

* If you had to choose which way your company leans on one side or the other, which is it?

* Do you like which way it leans? And if not, what kinds of things will you have to do differently to bridge that gap or balance it out if there is such a thing?

* Was I right in the introduction when I warned you I would mix metaphors and get wild with my analogies or is this all making sense to you? How upset would Dr. Chapman be right now?

Chapter 7

OVER-INDEXING ON ONE FORMAT

Shameless Admission

I debated including this chapter because I know I have a bias, and this would not only reveal it, but put it up on a giant pedestal with a spotlight, Roman candles going off on all sides, and a heavenly choir oohing in the background. However, even staying agnostic to product would still require I talk a lot about one medium differently than others for reasons you are about to see, so I decided to keep it and lean into it even harder. I'll show you why here, but let me get a match really quick so I can light these sparklers as I discuss it.

To show you what I am talking about let me share some recent national Nielsen media consumption data on adults in the United States and their time spent with electronic media.

Medium	Weekly Hours	Percentage
Traditional Live TV C time-shifted TV	18 hrs, 31 min	27.6%
Connected TV/Streaming	13 hrs, 44 min	20.4%
Radio	8 hrs, 54 min	13.3%
Internet on a PC	5 hrs, 7 min	7.6%
Internet or App on a Smartphone	18 hrs, 21 min	27.3%
Internet or App on a Tablet	3 hrs, 33 min	5.3%
Total Hours per week per person on average:	67 hrs, 10 min	101.5%*

*simultaneous multi-device usage in consumption makes this number add up to more than 100

First of all, let's shrug our shoulders and move on from the fact that more than half of our waking hours are spent with electronic media. After all, we've already determined that we lead stretched and distracted lives, with multiple priorities vying for our attention and advertising being a louder part of that. Also, one thing the list doesn't show is the growth of smartphones and streaming as part of the mix, at the expense of traditional live TV, broadcast and cable being the players suffering the most. There will be new information at publishing this that will show even more of it, but I took a slice of time. The summary is as I said, what's growing overall is the amount of media we consume. Quarter over quarter consumption grows again and again.

But when I look at this data, what jumps out to me most is how much of our consumption is video-related. Here is a list of ways video is included above:

-**Broadcast TV:** depending on the market, there are four or more local broadcast stations, with local news leading the way.

-**Cable TV:** all kinds of providers pipe content through a cable box. Comcast and Spectrum are the largest local providers, but depending on your area of the country, there are other great options that serve your community. You can watch TV on dozens of ad-supported and non-ad-supported channels.

-**Streaming TV options:** content is delivered via Smart devices or the tech is built into TVs (Smart TVs) without a cable subscription requirement. Netflix, Amazon, and Hulu, are some notable streaming options as well as a large host of FAST channels, named as such because they are Free Ad-Supported Television. Gaming is a newer streaming option emerging as well. We'll talk more about all of these for advertising later.

-**YouTube content**: both free and paid subscription content delivered on all kinds of devices. Where the others are delivered on the large screen most of the time, YouTube is very diverse in its device delivery, lending itself to taking up part of those "app/smartphone" delivery methods.

-**Social Media options:** in addition to organic and paid copy and static content, there is a wide range of video varieties for organic content creation as well as paid video options. Facebook C Instagram are widely popular, but TikTok and other channels ad hours to the daily viewing time, depending on what platforms cater to different demographics.

-**Movie Theatres:** often overlooked because it is an out-of-home experience, and it is much smaller in time spent per year, people are returning to the biggest screen for communal viewing of films. There is value in that shared experience and the size of the screen cannot be overlooked.

There are other options for video out there, video podcasts for example, but these listed are the main types of content that most drive the time spent upward. People of all ages are really into video and are hanging out in various types of video at every stage of their decision processes to buy what you sell.

Besides monopolizing leisure time, with more than six hours a day on average per person spent with it and climbing, video is ubiquitous at every stage of the purchase funnel. This means if you remain singularly focused in your messaging, which I promised you I would preach throughout this book, the video formats can more easily carry that message with clarity through the customer's journey to your door.

The final reason for making a chapter entirely devoted to video is that the power of its influence on behavior is unmatched by any other medium. Growth from Knowledge (GfK), one of the most respected consumer research companies and in the top 10 in the world, repeatedly share data that strongly supports video as the most capable of altering people's behavior of 20+ media platforms.

Perhaps interestingly, traditional broadcast and cable TV are the most influential of video platforms across the entire purchase funnel. What this means to you is that while advertisers have flocked to newfangled options that make headlines in the trades, at least for a season, there is tremendous power in taking what these advertisers have left behind. While using the values I will describe later that live in some of these newer video options, your ability to capitalize on the largest hype machines in the local market should not be ignored.

We can make another book out of why this phenomenon exists, but it might have something to do with the communal nature of broadcast and cable TV. Besides associating with trusted local or national media brands, these two types of video consumption have a big advantage when viewers know for sure that the experience can be shared by others. Word of mouth grows when it's possible the other person at the water cooler or PTA meeting has seen that show, that news item, or as with broadcast and cable, that ad that makes them look good for talking about it.

Intimate Experiences vs. Community Multipliers

When an ad appears on your home TV screen within a streaming environment, it is increasingly perceived, at least subconsciously, as being tailored specifically to you. This perception stems from the inherently personalized nature of streaming platforms, where the content is typically selected on-demand and watched on individual schedules. Unlike traditional live broadcast and cable TV, viewers are aware that others are likely watching entirely different content, on different timelines, and possibly on different devices. This context reinforces a sense that the ad experience is unique and intentionally targeted.

This sense of personalized experience intensifies as the viewing screen turns smaller, as with personal devices like smartphones or tablets. Pre-roll ads on these devices feel more intimate and individualized, reinforcing the assumption that they are meant for you alone. How likely are you to talk about that ad?

As you can see, this very intimacy can have a counterintuitive effect. Because the ad experience feels private, viewers may be less likely to discuss the ad in social settings. Research from Facebook and Nielsen has shown that shared ad experiences during live events drive higher conversation and brand lift. In contrast, the solitude of streaming often diminishes this social multiplier. This means that all video is not created equal, and how you use it should be optimized for this likely reality. When we get into helping you build your funnel, this is an important point and accentuates the imperative that each type of ad, on each type of device screen, in any environment, has to be judged by its unique capabilities and restrictions.

Before we move on, let's summarize this deep and powerful subject of video. Attention is great but it isn't just about attention, whether banking on time spent or volume of options in the journey. It's mostly about driving action and multiplying value. Recognizing that video has evolved and is now available in both complete and nuanced ways may seem difficult to grasp, but the effect of it can accelerate the inevitable if you get it right.

Think it Through

* What perceptions of video have you had and how have they changed based on this information?

* What kind of attention in your marketing have you placed on the video aspects of various platforms?

* If you've done video for advertising, how public or private have the placements been?

Chapter 8

FAMILIARITY SEEDS INTENT

A Party to Remember

Imagine being invited to a birthday party celebrating someone you know and like. The nature of your relationship with them is that it doesn't fit any other context of their lives. You are going to attend their party and are quite sure that the 100 other guests will be people you don't know. You care to see your friend, but it's likely you won't stay long because their attention will be monopolized by so many other guests for much of the time.

You arrive at the venue, place your gift on the receiving table, and enter a ballroom full of people. As expected, your friend is locked in conversation and won't be attending to you any time soon. You scan the room like you are taking it all in, but really you are looking for any other thing to do than just standing there alone. There are people everywhere. You aren't too introverted and want to meet new people, but waiting around for the interaction you came for might get awkward or quiet for you.

Suddenly, near the punch bowl, you see someone you have met before, and you are pretty sure the name of that person is Casey. You were introduced once briefly at another function. You've never spoken or seen each other beyond that one time. Your host today has mentioned this person in other contexts every once in a while. But other than vaguely recalling having met Casey, you have zero knowledge of anyone else in the room. Your eyes connect with Casey from across the room, and you both politely nod at each other like you have in fact met.

What are the chances that during the party you speak to Casey? What are the chances that you speak to Casey first? What are the chances that if you hit it off in the initial conversation that you only speak with Casey while you are waiting to see your friend during their party?

Statistically, the odds are high for all three potential outcomes, with at least speaking to Casey being 90-98% certainty, and only speaking to Casey (depending on your personality and relational style) about 50-65% certainty. You are going to be hanging out with Casey early, and quite possibly, you're only hanging out with Casey because this vague relationship has one thing no other guest in the room has with you: *familiarity.*

Awareness Feeds the Leads

Human behavior strongly favors seeking the familiar in unfamiliar settings. The fact that you made eye contact and nodded to each other is a mutual acknowledgment and an unspoken invitation. Casey is an anchor in a high-friction environment, and your likely interaction with them reveals a massive truth about Awareness Media.

When mass media creates awareness, it can also bypass the journey sometimes and create a connection that moves immediately to a generated lead, depending on factors we will discuss in a later chapter. What Awareness does best is to create the familiarity required to gain an advantage of connection when someone is finally in that 5% of the market that is ready to buy.

All the ad products I am about to list and discuss are best used to build this familiarity in the future customers who are still in the 95% of the market who are not ready or interested yet.

The metaphorical party the consumer is attending is a search engine results page, where they can scan what's there and give you a nod of acknowledgment from across the internet by way of a phone call, form fill, or in-person visit. You are their light connection, and that's all it takes in a crowded room of the unfamiliar to have them at least give you a chance to get acquainted.

If Awareness Media can do that, Consideration and especially Intent have a much better chance of converting more leads.

Your advantage here is that many advertisers can't or won't build enough familiarity in the 95% of the market, and that will make

them take a back seat to you when and if a search engine results page is ready to attempt the conversion.

In order of widest reach and narrowing as you climb, here are the demographic, geographic, and psychographic-driven media available to you in the local market and a primer on each.

As you will see, some of the products as the list narrows, can also be used well in other parts of the funnel so long as you have enough coverage beforehand. This will be true about other products in future chapters.

Local Broadcast Television. With the widest reach of both sight and sound of any media, local broadcast is split up amongst several national brands with local affiliates.

Best Used When:

1. Your offer is both eligible for and requires the entire designated market area (DMA) and your dependence on customers from a wide radius is essential to your business. This does not mean that just because you CAN reach outside your typical service area also means you SHOULD. Cost analysis on what a customer is worth should help you easily solve the dilemma of leaving potential customers out if the geography is too difficult to reach and another TV choice fits better for the area you are pursuing.

2. When you need the ultimate brand play, associating with local news ads to the influence that TV provides.
3. Your product or service tends to sell well to the masses who represent an older demographic. You can't limit it to just them, but broadcast reaches that demo quite easily.

Avoid When:

1. Your message requires tighter targeting than the entire DMA and all demographics.
2. Your budget isn't robust for the industry or you aren't perched for growth.

Strengths:

- Credibility of local news.
- High impact for brand recall.

Weaknesses:

- Expensive and wasteful for niche audiences.
- Harder to track directly compared to digital media.
- Increasingly less audience than there used to be.

Common Pitfalls:

- Underestimating the need for strong creative to stand out.
- Overusing it for lower-funnel or hyperlocal campaigns.

Strategic Opportunities:

- Use as a halo medium to drive more interactivity in consideration media where more time is offered.

- Leverage news sponsorships or weather triggers to align with relevant content.

Role Play:

Riley – With only one location and a reduced ad budget, Riley knows this ad product might need to be eliminated for something that behaves similarly without all the waste. There might be a local tie-in on something if there is enough budget left, but her cost to acquire a customer will possibly go up just to have the association.

Chris – With a unique message that a luxury brand is only available at his furniture store, Chris should definitely consider broadcast TV, depending on the income level in various communities within the footprint. He can beef up with something else in the funnel in the most affluent areas, but speaking with all the major stations is a good idea.

Vanessa – With a service like HVAC, and trucks capable of rolling out and easily serving all over the DMA, Vanessa's usage of Broadcast TV is critical to her success. She might even choose multiples if she can see unduplicated reach bringing even more value. Beating the bigger players in the market might also mean sponsoring segments of local news opportunities within content.

Radio - AM/FM. As the medium with the highest reach of adults and the best cost efficiency for any awareness ad product, local radio stations have a wide variety of formats.

Best Used When:

1. You are buying other awareness media and want to put a frequency multiplier on it. With regularly 3x-5x more impressions per dollar than broadcast or digital video ads, radio delivers extremely low CPMs. If you want frequency and are budget-conscious, radio has anchoring capabilities for scale.

2. You want to reflect or guide local culture. Radio has personalities, news, events and energy that advertisers can easily utilize if they have a cultural narrative that needs to feel local and set a community expectation into their messaging without having to be heavy-handed with it.

3. You want versatility and flexibility to get creative, as writing, producing and airing can be done within 48-72 hours. Radio gives an advertiser the right to get to the heart of a person emotionally much easier.

Avoid When:

1. You need visual storytelling for the product or service you are describing to be understood clearly.

2. You don't need working-class or blue-collar commuters as well as parents with children.

Strengths:

- Because screens are not part of the ad experience, it is an unduplicated reach when added to other awareness, extending its value.
- Flexible pricing, strong community connection.
- Excellent for frequency and message reinforcement.

Weaknesses:

- Lacks attribution metrics for sales like TV, while some of their digital yet much smaller digital counterparts can.
- Often undervalued in multi-channel strategies (but this is an opportunity for the marketer who is diligent).

Common Pitfalls:

- Running vague, generic ads with no frequency plan or peddling product and pricing.
- Neglecting proper voice talent, production quality or the chance to use brand-imaged music for other audio applications.

Strategic Opportunities:

- Sponsor local personalities or programs for deeper brand trust.
- Pair with social or search for consideration and intent-layered messaging.
- Bolster events with a concentrated blitz.

Role Play:

Riley – Banking on what she determined when she decided what the company's unique promise that can be delivered is, Riley could easily write highly emotion-driven radio ads that connect with the hard-working and generally younger radio audience.

For example: "People making decisions about your loans are local. You aren't just an account number with us. You're our neighbor, and that familiarity is special for you."

Chris – Knowing that luxury purchases are rarely rational and highly emotional, radio might be a great fit for him. Particularly if the furniture needed to tell the market about their pivot to luxury, he could speak to that audience on something other than price, except for the "everything cheap must go" sale to signal the pivot.

Vanessa – With her size and scale, she also has an opportunity to utilize radio to keep a large company feeling more approachable and local.

The lure of being everywhere is strong, but the idea that maybe splitting some broadcast money off to radio to amplify reach inexpensively might just be the way to be everywhere her future customers might live.

Major Out of Home (OOH) / Billboard. Billboards that loom over roadways have an imposing, larger-than-life presence, and can significantly amplify other awareness advertising because it is among the most public experiences.

Best Used When:

1. You want high-visibility, unavoidable local presence. As discussed in the section about video, related to intimate experiences vs. communal multipliers, large billboards support the idea articulated by Jonah Berger in his book,

Contagious, "Built to show, built to grow." People talk about things they know others are also seeing.

2. You want the quickest awareness for big announcements or triggering impulses to reach drivers in high-traffic zones. Because these drivers are reached repeatedly, it's quite easy to influence short-term decisions in the awareness space.

3. You want brand reinforcement in specific geographic areas that are repeated to make you feel like you are "everywhere."

Avoid When:

1. You have a long, complex message that requires educating the consumer well first.

2. Your business doesn't have a local physical or service footprint.

Strengths:

- 24/7 exposure, geographic control.
- Great for brand reinforcement and recall in which.

Weaknesses:

- No interactivity or immediate attribution.
- Creative space is limited—can be wasteful if poorly designed.
- Short viewing time.

Common Pitfalls:

- Cramming too much text or detail into small formats.
- Forgetting to rotate or refresh creative.

Strategic Opportunities:

- Use as a directional signal if your location lacks intrusive visibility but is conducive to drop-by impulse interactions.
- Combine with digital retargeting ads to add another layer of visibility on mobile devices or social ads.
- If what you say can be done in 7 words or less, preferably 3 words, it works well.

Role Play:

Riley – With only one location near the heart of town but close to the highway, Riley might do well to get a billboard on each side of their exit, reinforcing the message being delivered on other media.

She'll need to convey a concise version of that, like "Local People. Local Loans."

Perhaps "Right on First Street" below it or something with the logo. For budget, this might be a small but impactful use of the larger-than-life presence that billboards offer.

Chris – If he can identify the affluent neighborhoods and they are available nearby, Chris can sell taste, status, and credibility with a looming board. A sign in a prestigious font that shows the luxury brand name and "only at," and the logo, he might just reinforce the other media he does targeting that neighborhood.

Vanessa – Knowing that she will have urgency calls due to weather, Vanessa can use some boards to roll with those seasons, particularly in locations where there are older homes and likely older units for maintenance and change out. She is budgeted right, so perhaps a few around home improvement stores speaking to DIY'ers that perhaps they should just call Vanessa's company.

Cable TV. As an accouterment to broader reach ad products, cable serves as a tightening of geography and demographics of broadcast, while maintaining the duplicity of the largesse of well-known media brands with the hyper-local footprint of the denser population.

Best Used When:

1. You want to boost frequency in an area of town more suited to your location and the radius customers would normally come from. While the reach is much lower than broadcast or radio, the validated reach means frequency can remain high on a modest budget.
2. You want to reduce waste by selecting only cable networks that index high for your product or service. Set-top box data can be utilized to hyper-focus on viewers that more likely to be your customers.
3. You want to associate your company with a well-known TV brand or show without having to pay larger scale prices to get it.

Avoid When:

1. Too much of your footprint has cut the cord, and the cable provider doesn't have a viable streaming option.
2. You need high production value on a tiny budget, as they will more times than not have to outsource some or all of the production work, increasing the cost to produce good ads.

Strengths:

- Zone-targeting, dayparting, and flexibility of high-profile national sports and news at a local buying level.
- Still strong reach among older audiences and homeowners.

Weaknesses:

- Limited reach in streaming-heavy households.
- Viewer attention is often fragmented.

Common Pitfalls:

- Assuming cable is just as expensive as broadcast TV because the cost to obtain a more likely viewer is higher.
- Not using the cable company's first-party data to support audience targeting where ratings don't match up to the scale of broadcast TV.

Strategic Opportunities:

- Great testing ground for TV during geographical expansion beyond the basic digital advertising being done but not the giant leap required to the larger mass media products.

- Can pair with streaming to gain reach and frequency well under one strategic plan and one buy with one company.

Role Play:

Riley – As a TV opportunity, cable presents itself as a great first chance to feel large scale of awareness media. She'll have to get geographically specific to the area's cable TV zone alignment, but Riley can get a frequency within her customer area that makes sense. She can appear as though she is everywhere to her target without having to spend too much of the budget.

Chris – Looking at the cable zones and set-top box data indexing, Chris can reach the affluent viewers geographically and demographically. Coupling the cable with some of the other awareness options will give his customers regular top-of-mind recall that if you want furniture luxury, this is the place to go. Perhaps some fixed position ads that align on a psychographic level like an HGTV show would go further.

Vanessa – Using her internal CRM system, Vanessa can select tighter audiences based on where their well-branded trucks are already spending a lot of time. Allowing her own data to inform the decision will make it easier to gain the attribution requests of her CEO.

Digital OOH. Out of Home signage has more versatility and perceived dominance when it is displayed electronically over the roadways. Otherwise behaving like static boards, DOOH has unique differences in execution.

Best Used When:

1. You want dynamic, rotating creative in high-traffic digital signage areas. If your creative messages might have to change more frequently than a standard board should have for effect, DOOH is a good way to keep the messaging fresh without paying as much to produce the ad because there is no materials to print or labor needed to install.

2. You want geo-targeted messages with time-sensitive messaging. Of course, you will be restricted to where digital boards are available, but it the geography makes sense, and you have something to offer with a sense of urgency on it, DOOH might be a good fit as one of the closest options to intent within the awareness funnel.

3. You want a lower CPM for awareness than other electronic media with the perception of "video". Digital billboards aren't exactly the same experience, but they maintain their public nature and feel like video but with a fraction of the video CPMs, similar to that of radio, for that kind of scale.

Avoid When:

1. You can't afford frequent updates due to internal time constraints.

2. You need long-term exposure without re-buying impressions.

Strengths:

- Flexible scheduling, rotating creatives.

- Attention-grabbing due to motion/digital animation.

Weaknesses:

- Limited dwell time to process messages.
- Can be pricey compared to static boards for the same footprint.

Common Pitfalls:

- Repeating static creative designed for print in digital format.
- Not optimizing message timing or location relevance.

Strategic Opportunities:

- Great for countdowns, flash sales, or teaser campaigns.
- Sync with mobile retargeting for seamless experience.

Role Play:

Riley – A large scale digital board might give the illusion of budget and share of market on a lower budget, but if none are available, she might have to stick with the static boards near her location's exits as previously shared.

If she's clever, however, she might see if a digital board is available where her management or board commutes from and buy one to remind them that ads work. Bonus points if she uses digital photography of the local decision makers in the ads, which will behave differently than the directional ads but not work counter to the plan but not require a ton of reset work if it is not well-received.

Chris – Seeing that a DOOH large board can underscore the idea of value subtly, he might benefit from product-specific ads on some of the best margined products in the new line. Also, he could start creative to run the fire sale of the other lines of product to make room for the brand change and do a countdown to the rebrand perhaps.

Vanessa – All Vanessa needs to do is consider what difference it makes to add another layer of low CPM ads but for significant budget. Her best option might be to have something evergreen up but as soon as there is a weather event that triggers HVAC needs, changing the creative on the fly to address cold or heat issues that are more likely to occur.

Paid Social Ads. With the tightest, most intent-like offer inside awareness media options, Social Ads run on the world's most known platforms typically, Facebook and Instagram. While other options exist, the most notable are these, both owned by parent company, Meta.

Best Used When:

1. You want to target by interest, behavior, or customize an audience. Social media options can become extremely versatile in the customization process, but as with any media, your willingness to pay more to get it is key.
2. You have a specific action you want them to take, even if it is not a short-term offer. The ability to behave in long and

short-term ways to an audience that likely does not yet know or follow you within social media. You can create both followers for the long haul or immediate conversions, depending on what kind of ads you run.

3. You want the convenience of testing ad units, messaging, and other mechanisms to inform other media choices. Call to Action (CTA) buttons andcarousel, video, or static options can be tested in real time to determine quick adaptations of the creative elements.

Avoid When:

1. Paid reach is unnecessary due to organic post engagement and more awareness media and the website has driven more social proof traffic.
2. The nuance of your message is not suited to short-scroll attention spans.

Strengths:

- Micro-targeting, A/B testing, visual storytelling.
- Direct engagement and shareability are better than traditional awareness media due to social's environment.

Weaknesses:

- Constant platform and algorithm changes keeps you regularly having to test and adapt.
- Creative rotation is key, as ad fatigue on this platform happens much faster.

Common Pitfalls:

- Over-targeting leads to small audiences and high costs.
- Ignoring creative quality or CTA strength.

Strategic Opportunities:

- Use lookalike audiences and remarketing to scale successful campaigns.
- Run lead-gen campaigns tied to CRM/email nurturing.
- Use as connective tissue to consideration media where awareness budget is sparse.

Role Play:

Riley – To address budget concerns, she might do well to study what Facebook can get her bank access to related to certain kinds of targets that are auto intenders that may need a loan, or perhaps audiences in a geographic and demographic type that also is known to shop locally. With many anonymized options to consider, Riley will at least have some opportunities to make her other media force the leads through to consideration phase with strategic placements.

Chris – Finding audiences both in the short term where all the non-luxury items "must go" as well as a second campaign targeting those who would likely shop the luxury brand, Chris can manage two separate campaigns and easily build ads to test and turn off budget based on effectiveness or completion of the initiative.

Vanessa – Reinforcing various geographies and perhaps a homeowner audience specifically, Vanessa can run a campaign throughout the time of year the wallets would be open for HVAC services. Various promotions around generators and other co-op provided by manufacturers might give an extension to the brand and specific leads.

Other Awareness Options. Use each of these based on their level of deeper intimacy, despite their lack of scale that awareness generates. Done well, any of these can create even more touches to guide leads into belief that bypasses the need to be focused on price competitiveness. Proceed cautiously but optimistically.

Streaming Audio

Best Used When:

- Reaching digital-first audiences (Spotify, Pandora, podcasts).
- Complementing digital video and paid social.

Avoid When:

- You need trackable clicks or immediate conversions.
- Your budget is tight, as CPMs can be high without volume.

Strengths:

- Targetable by behavior, genre, location.
- High engagement during focused listening.

Weaknesses:

- Largely not clickable, therefore harder to measure intent.
- Needs excellent audio production as listeners tend to listen with more sophisticated speakers or headphones.

Common Pitfalls:

- Using traditional radio ads instead of tailored digital spots.
- Forgetting to put the brand specifically in first few seconds.

Strategic Opportunities:

- Target by mood or activity (e.g., "workout" playlists or podcasts).
- Use companion banners for secondary engagement.

Pre-Roll Video

Best Used When:

- Supporting a clear offer or action-based message in a short, memorable hook.
- Targeting at the household level like streaming can.

Avoid When:

- Using non-skippable formats when the video is longer than 15 seconds.
- Running the same message everywhere without platform nuance.

Strengths:

- Strong storytelling in short bursts.
- Clickable, trackable, and measurable.

Weaknesses:

- Ad fatigue if creative is not rotated or updated similar to what happens in the social media environment.
- Completion rates vary by platform and audience.

Common Pitfalls:

- Front-loading branding instead of hooking attention.
- Treating pre-roll like TV when it carries a different length and pacing.

Strategic Opportunities:

- Pair with YouTube keyword targeting or behavioral retargeting.
- Use skippable ads to tease curiosity and drive click-throughs.

Cinema Ads

Best Used When:

- You want undivided attention in a premium visual environment.
- Promoting local lifestyle brands, events, or prestige products.

Avoid When:

- You need a quick response or measurable clicks.
- Your audience does not include frequent moviegoers.

Strengths:

- Full-screen, high-impact message delivery.
- Repeated weekly impressions to loyal viewers.

Weaknesses:

- Slow turnaround on changes.
- Audience reach limited to current moviegoers.

Common Pitfalls:

- Using static or low-quality video in a cinematic setting.
- Misjudging audience size and demo.

Strategic Opportunities:

- Use to build "brand aura" in upper funnel.

- Combine with QR codes or short URL prompts for follow-up or lead capture.

Local Newspaper

Best Used When:

- Reaching older or local community-engaged readers.
- Supporting coupons, schedules, a calendar of events, legal notices, or editorial adjacencies.

Avoid When:

- Targeting young or digital-first audiences.
- Relying on it as the only awareness vehicle.

Strengths:

- Trusted source, longer shelf life for inserts.
- Local relevance and contextual alignment.

Weaknesses:

- Declining readership, low engagement from digital natives.
- Production timelines may slow down speed to market.

Common Pitfalls:

- Placing in poor sections with low visibility.
- Using cluttered, text-heavy layouts.

Strategic Opportunities:

- Pair print with digital e-edition sponsorship.
- Buy placements near relevant content (e.g., real estate, autos).

Local Magazines

Best Used When:

- Appealing to upscale or niche lifestyle audiences.
- Building prestige or aligning with aspirational content.

Avoid When:

- Seeking high-frequency, high-reach exposure.
- Your brand doesn't align with the editorial tone.

Strengths:

- Beautiful, high-quality presentation.
- Long shelf life in homes, waiting rooms, salons.

Weaknesses:

- Long lead times.
- Limited issues per year means fewer touchpoints.

Common Pitfalls:

- Misjudging the actual readership size or demo.
- Overinvesting for limited ROI.

Strategic Opportunities:

- Great for image-based businesses (design, luxury, wellness).
- Leverage content partnerships or advertorials for added trust-building.

Local Sponsorships / Neighborhood Events

Best Used When:

- You want to be "seen" in the community and build goodwill.
- Engaging hyper-local audiences (PTA, chamber events, youth sports, etc.).

Avoid When:

- You're seeking measurable, immediate ROI.
- You're not able to follow through with presence or activation.

Strengths:

- Builds community trust and emotional connection.
- Often affordable and personal.

Weaknesses:

- Reach is limited, inconsistent, and regularly unpredictable.
- Can be time-consuming without clear lead capture.

Common Pitfalls:

- Just slapping your logo on something with no follow-up.
- Skipping event presence and interaction. Empty tables or tents that have your company brand on them work against your goal, and you will have paid for that loss twice.

Strategic Opportunities:

- Collect leads or social followers at events.
- Use photos and recaps as social proof, as well as hashtags or tagging on your organic social media pages.

Direct Mail (at scale)

Best Used When:

- Targeting households by geography, income, or behavior.
- Promoting specific offers, coupons, or calls to action.

Avoid When:

- Your message is too brand-focused with no clear CTA.
- You're unwilling to test and iterate.

Strengths:

- Tangible, targeted, and trackable.
- Can feel more personal than digital.

Weaknesses:

- Rising postage and printing costs.
- Low response without great creative or list strategy.

Common Pitfalls:

- Using outdated or unfiltered lists.
- Ignoring QR codes or digital tie-ins.

Strategic Opportunities:

- Combine with digital retargeting to create more touches at the household level.
- A/B test offers, formats, and timing for optimization.

Awareness in Perspective

From the length of this section, and the power of the reach and frequency these products offer, you'd think that this is where all the money goes locally, but this is not the case. Due to the fact that the different versions of the funnel I mentioned early in the book create different ways to designate how the money is spent in that funnel, there are inconsistent metrics about where the money goes in each bucket; however, most research suggests that Awareness Media options that plant seeds of familiarity and not a conversion metric only receive about 28% of the budget. While there are some Consideration Media options that act like Awareness and can bring that number up slightly, the vast majority of local dollars are placed in other media options than awareness.

Your distinct advantage in this space that fewer advertisers take advantage of the opportunity, first because of the incorrect assumption it's too expensive for not being able to track easily, particularly with click metric volume and attribution assumptions, but also because the ad-buying public who has followed the headlines and not thought very deeply have abandoned an important fact about relationships that stick: a torrid love affair that culminates in a successful marriage starts with an introduction followed by time spent together in one form of media or another. And none of those forms are products or tactics that constantly pops the question.

In reality, the proposal gets captured on video, but how it got there usually requires a long, complex set of situations of growing together, and these moments are built in private and typically not captured for all to see. These quiet yet foundational moments that made the decision to unite and seal it with a ring are what make it an easy "Yes, I'll marry you." Marketers who want the "Yes" and want to keep the commitment going also know that short term tactics and ad products don't create these long-term relationships going. I'll say more of this later, but the opportunity to own share of mind for the time is right is an advantage waiting for you to take it.

Think it Through

* Have you been concentrating on the 5% in the market right now when you place ads? Why do you think that is?

* What kind of pressure on price have you experienced when using awareness media types compared to intent media pricing pressures? Have you seen a notable difference?

* What perceptions of mass media used for building awareness have changed in you?

Chapter 9

VERIFY FIRST VS. TRUST FIRST

Mikey Likes It

In 1972, long before internet chat rooms, listing sites, online message boards, social apps, or Google reviews, Life Cereal aired what would become one of the most iconic TV ads of the decade. The commercial featured two young boys with anxiety over trying the new cereal. In their thick Bronx accents, the pair decides to see if a third boy, Mikey, would eat from the bowl, stating, "Let's get Mikey! He won't try it; he hates everything!"

Of course, Mikey liked it, and a classic was born. Little Mikey unwittingly showed parents and kids that a cereal that's good for you can also taste good. Whether it's a new breakfast item or a mobile tire repair service advertising to us, we have the need for social proofing wired into us when confronted with uncertainty and risk after familiarity has begun. The greater the potential of improbability of a claim, the more proof we require, especially when safety, security, and finances are involved.

And just to keep the full focus of my underlying point of this book staying clear throughout, it's a good time to remind you that the remedy for potential improbability isn't to say more in your ad to cover all bases or to lower the promise to reduce doubt. You'll either wash out your singular message on one hand, or sound like everyone else on the other. Neither of those will get you leads. You will bleed money. If skepticism about a brand's claim is potentially high, peer-to-peer evaluation and recommendation is essential to keeping the lead from stalling out during the consumer's journey.

When the information age took off in the late 90s, access to social proof became a much larger cultural element. Why? For starters, the internet unlocked scale for validation or invalidation of a brand, as it opened people to the opinions of real customers rather than just the ones they knew. Secondly, at the same time, trust in media began to decline, as so many outlets began to cater programming to their audience's bias rather than just report the news. This caused a perceived asymmetry in what we can know beyond reasonable doubt, forcing the need for more proof than ever before. What we have now is a spectrum of news for every belief system, not every belief system given the facts to use critical thinking to evaluate beliefs on their own.

These cultural moments accelerated distrust, and scandal after scandal that was now more likely to be reported on poured high-octane fuel on a smoldering pile of rubbish. We now walk very carefully through what we observe, even with trusted companions, because danger of making bad conclusions could cost us at every turn. The best thing to redeem any of that possibly for an advertiser, is the chance to build social proof through advertising options built specifically but perhaps not intentionally to serve this need to verify, then trust.

A New Hope

Social proof can be defined broadly as any media, paid, owned, earned or shared, that provides a potential customer with more touches of information to reinforce awareness from multiple angles. To be clear, it isn't just how the media platforms are built, but how they function in the mind of the prospective customer. They are the connective tissue between familiarity and conversion; they are the lingering conversations that provide your future customers peace that you are worthy of that long-term relationship. If you pay enough attention to your brand's proof-offering mechanisms, you will spend less money overall because you have provided so many ways to believe in you that intent media is even less necessary. Until we get to that, grab yourself a bowl of cereal, and let's look at all the main players of consideration media.

Display Ads (Geo/Demo Targeting). Online version of billboards appears above, below, or on the side of content with the upgrade of clicking the ad through to a designated website of the advertiser.

Best Used When:

1. You want to reinforce brand validity to a potential customer who is likely already in the market or whose online behavior fits into an archetype desired by the advertiser. Device IDs and IP Addresses in the home contain anonymized data advertisers can use to add a layer of targeting these potential customers.

2. You want to target by geography or demographics to keep your name in the buyer's decision set when other media have built some familiarity. Using less customer data offers a typically lower CPM when geo and demo targets are the only filters you set.

3. You have an offer that lends itself to impulse and a lower threshold of consideration financially to say yes. The higher the mental acuity to deciding, the worse display performs on click-throughs.

Avoid When:

1. You haven't built any trust signals yet. Display's value plummets when it has to act as its own awareness tool.
2. You don't have a specific frequency plan in place. Capping the amount of times one user can be served in a day, a week, or a month will keep from annoying them.

Strengths:

- Follows the user across their browsing journey, creating a "popular and relevant" perception.
- Can include testimonials, awards, ratings in creative for proof reinforcement.

Weaknesses:

- Ad fatigue if creative is not varied.
- Click-throughs don't always mean serious interest.

Common Pitfalls:

- Using generic branding without any social proof elements.
- Forgetting to test creative featuring reviews or customer quotes.

Strategic Opportunities:

- Rotate ad creative featuring top customer reviews, press quotes, or certifications.
- Pair retargeting with timed offers to prompt action before competitors.

Role Play:

Riley – With a leadership team being possibly asked to let marketing do a lot that isn't like it used to be, centered on rates and special offers, Riley can extend her awareness with offers available through display ads, while targeting them down to the community right around where she is

already advertising. If budget allows she could also consider an auto intender receiving an auto loan ad and other possibilities with the targeting.

Chris – Extending frequency to his awareness buy, Chris can narrow his focus to the affluent neighborhoods his large billboards attempt to reach. The smaller screen in the home on a desktop, tablet, or mobile device can put a twist on the luxury promise with a clickable action like scheduling a private showing or being on a list that gets exclusive offers via another channel like email, text, etc.

Vanessa – Having planned and executed a lot of awareness while in growth mode, Vanessa can use display to build credibility by offering something that triggers proof without paying for it. Perhaps a free assessment of your HVAC system, or free filter change. Something that lets a prospect try before they buy and let them get proof that way.

OOH – (Medium-Sized Bulletin Boards G Place-Based Signage). Unlike its imposing counterparts, street level boards and signage on benches, bus stops, and train platforms can offer an unspoken intimacy and relatability and personalize the experience.

Best Used When:

1. You want to reinforce credibility by appearing in high-traffic local spaces (gym, transit, shopping areas). Special attention should be paid to the type of customer that frequents these locations so that your specific desired customer can see you.
2. You are supporting the "trusted choice" positioning in familiar community environments. Consider creative that is the effect of the promise when the awareness media is sufficiently stating the cause of the promise.

Avoid When:

1. You need highly detailed messaging as dwell time is short.
2. Your business is not geographically relevant to the location.

Strengths:

- Visibility in local "daily life" spaces builds the sense you're an established, trusted local brand.
- Can feature recognizable local faces better than larger boards.

Weaknesses:

- Limited space for proof-heavy content.
- Reach is highly dependent on location quality.

Common Pitfalls:

- Choosing locations without target audience alignment.
- Cluttering small formats with too much text.

Strategic Opportunities:

- Use boards to show off other social proof like Google ratings or customer satisfaction scores.
- Add QR codes linking to reviews or testimonials.

Role Play:

Riley – Having a budget-friendly alternative to the larger boards, Riley might be able to play off the intimacy of the smaller boards and place-based ads to keep the rate-conscious consumer still engaged in possibly using her bank. Also, the option of using local faces in leadership can extend the look and feel of the electronic media that used those same faces.

Chris – Taking a closer look at place-based ads of outdoor shopping malls near other higher-end brands might be Chris' best use of this media. He could also consider similar options at the airport, where he could extend the luxury feel the likelihood of the air traveler being someone whom "first class seating" could find more credible at home.

Vanessa – Perhaps boosting belief with contractors who would hire her company to do new construction installs, Vanessa might consider doing small boards near where builders get their supplies or near entrances to neighborhoods they are already doing new builds. The messaging would obviously cater to the contractor or even the new home buyers that they are getting an upgrade in this neighborhood.

Review Sites. Perhaps the most important factor in social proofing, the internet is chock full of sites that contain listings and reviews of local businesses.

Best Used When:

1. Your category and/or pricing models require validation before purchase and typically not a often-repeated purchase. If much has changed since the last time they bought, they likely won't have a loyalty to anyone, including you.
2. You have a customer base that is or would become raving fans of your work, particularly by meeting or exceeding the promises you have made to the public. You are notably better than the competition.
3. You want to leverage platforms like Google Business Profile, Yelp, TripAdvisor, Angi, Zillow, Healthgrades, or other niche-specific sites to your industry, of which there are dozens.

Avoid When:

1. You have unresolved customer service issues that keep ratings low.
2. You cannot maintain active monitoring and response.

Strengths:

- Social proof is explicit: star ratings, testimonials, volume of reviews of REAL customers with no incentive to steer you wrong or even know you are considering.
- Often ranks high organically in branded search, influencing even unplanned visits.

Weaknesses:

- Vulnerable to negative reviews.
- Competitors are one click away as they are listed nearby on most review/listing sites.

Common Pitfalls:

- Failing to respond promptly to reviews (both positive and negative).
- Asking for reviews only sporadically instead of making it part of the process.

Strategic Opportunities:

- Use high-scoring reviews in ad creative (display, OOH, social).
- Create "as seen on" graphics highlighting review site recognition.

Role Play:

Riley – With so much equity built in many years of business before Riley, the bank has many positive reviews that outrank the negatives by a wide margin. She can begin responding to those reviews, starting with the most recent and personalize the experience. It will also signal to future customers that the bank cares about its customers.

Chris – the pivot to luxury gives Chris a tremendous opportunity to comb through reviews and respond to comments specifically where he can address the changes coming to or recently made by the company. He can also update all listings to reflect the changes.

Vanessa – Because at some point, the volume of reviews matters more when the overall ratings are similarly close to 5 stars, she'll likely need to have the team look at how and at what point reviews are solicited and set a plan to bring consistency of requesting new customer reviews as well as working in tandem with the CRM tool to reach back to previous customers who were satisfied but did not leave a review.

Organic Social Media. As another owned and earned medium in social spaces, platforms like Facebook and Instagram serve to let future customers linger by scrolling your page or get updates by becoming a subscriber.

Best Used When:

1. You want to build an authentic, relatable brand image through consistent content and community interaction. By illustrating your promises kept after making them in other

media, prospects can both build belief and become a conduit for others' belief through their interactivity.

2. You want to showcase real customers, testimonials, and behind-the-scenes moments. Aggregating these real experiences lends credibility to your brand because you are sharing what others say as a means of saying it yourself.

3. You want to make sure any special offer is available to your followers and fans without having to pay extra to reach them with a short-term initiative.

Avoid When:

1. You would rather treat it like a replacement for your website or as a static brochure with no conversation.

2. You would post sporadically with no recognizable brand voice or identifiable purpose in the conversation.

3. You would use the platform for personal beliefs not reflective of the brand's promise, or if those are your business's beliefs and you are intentionally using the platform to signal discrimination against another group of people.

Strengths:

- Enables proof through visible engagement: comments, shares, tagged customer posts.
- Allows for real-time trust-building interactions.

Weaknesses:

- Reach is algorithm-limited without boosting. Unless it is deemed good for the platform, organic reach is highly throttled.
- It can backfire if negative feedback is visible and unaddressed.

Common Pitfalls:

- Only posting promotions instead of proof-driven storytelling.
- Ignoring user-generated content opportunities.

Strategic Opportunities:

- Spotlight customer stories, before/after transformations, or media features.
- Use social proof by association: tag partners, influencers, or reputable organizations.

Role Play:

Riley – To humanize the bank and convey local decision-making, Riley can spotlight long-standing employees and post each at regular intervals. Additionally, she can post regularly about financial tips that followers could comment on or share, particularly tips that don't require the compliance department to alter or decline the idea.

Chris – Using organic social media to build interest, Chris can show customer photos of upgraded spaces after delivery and set up, tell their followers when new items have arrived, or film a testimonial video of an upscale customer who outfitted their entire space using Chris's luxury lines.

Vanessa – In an industry not typically associated with anything dynamic, and having her own social media employee, Vanessa can get out of the static social proof and give flavor to the brand that large competitors aren't giving. Perhaps they can use employees to film parodies of pop culture that insert the brand and industry into the narrative and make people want to share it for its clever humor.

Email Marketing (External Lists). When extending reach in other platforms, emailing potential customers with news they can use can significantly advance the belief or relationship.

Best Used When:

1. You want to build trust with those you fill a need for who likely have heard of you but have not opted-into anything with you that you know of. Speaking their language is important, and you can signal you can do so by making THEM the hero of their story and you are the guide.

2. You want to share reviews, case studies, success stories, and third-party endorsements. It won't matter that you sent it as an advertising endeavor as much as it will matter

what they can learn about you to advance trust through great information.

Avoid When:

1. Blasting generic offers without relationship, or at the very least, segmentation.
2. Open and click metrics are more important to you than the value of the touch.

Strengths:

- Owned channel with high control over message and visuals.
- Ideal for delivering proof in specific contexts.

Weaknesses:

- Requires a healthy, permission-based list.
- Open rates can suffer without strong subject lines.

Common Pitfalls:

- Burying proof elements deep in the email instead of featuring them at the top.
- Using overly stock-looking imagery that undermines authenticity.

Strategic Opportunities:

- Dedicate entire sends to social proof themes ("What our customers are saying this month").

- Incorporate media logos or "as featured in" strips in email templates.

Local Influencer Marketing / Local Celebrity Endorsements. Perhaps overlooked because scaled influencers don't fit the geography, local icons can pull both awareness and consideration for very little effort.

Best Used When:

1. You want to borrow the trust, personality, and following of a known figure in the community.
2. Your product/service aligns with the influencer's lifestyle or authority.

Avoid When:

1. The influencer's audience doesn't match your target demo.
2. You can't verify their credibility or reputation, or the possibility of their reputation becoming polarized.

Strengths:

- Social proof by association saying essentially, "If they trust it, so should I."
- Often creates relatable, authentic content.

Weaknesses:

- Dependent on the influencer's current popularity and trust.

- Tracking return on spend can be tricky to quantify, especially if many media initiatives are running at once.

Common Pitfalls:

- Selecting based solely on follower count instead of engagement and community standing.
- Over-scripted endorsements that feel inauthentic.

Strategic Opportunities:

- Leverage influencer-created content across your paid and owned channels.
- Partner for live appearances or co-hosted community events.

Role Play:

Riley – Seeing him in the lobby one day hanging out with a VP of client services, Riley learns that a famous novelist banks at her bank. Leveraging the bank's relationship with him might give her better attendance at community events she sponsors, perhaps activating a book signing. As long as FTC and SEC regulations are followed, the applications of this endorsement are extensive.

Chris – Attempting to weave the luxury lines of furniture narrative into the brand, Chris might consider an endorsement shared on all media outlets depicting the city's famous college basketball coach in one of their easy chairs. Known for his large salary, his presence signals to others that if you are wealthy, you have this furniture from this store.

Vanessa – As part of her large Broadcast TV plan as leverage, Vanessa could convince the local station with the most market's most recognizable meteorologist to tie a clever narrative into ads that discusses weather-related concerns as a means of reminding homeowners to have Vanessa's company repair or replace their systems before the weather turns harsh.

Other Consideration Options. Use each of these based on how well they tie together other forms of media to bridge the gap between knowing of and buying from. Done well, your company can provide more proof to future customers and good reminders to those who need to be put back into the purchase funnel.

CRM Targeting (Email or Text)

Best Used When:

- Reaching people who have an established relationship or transaction history and can be resold or upsold.
- Delivering personalized proof that's relevant to their past behavior.

Avoid When:

- You lack clean, segmented data.
- Your database is small and inactive.

Strengths:

- First-party data allows for highly targeted trust reinforcement.
- Can deliver proof matched to customer lifecycle stage as with "most popular upgrade" style messages.

Weaknesses:

- Requires strong database health and integration.
- Easy to over-message and cause fatigue if not well timed or paced.

Common Pitfalls:

- Sending generic messaging without personalization.
- Neglecting opt-out and compliance rules.

Strategic Opportunities:

- Share customer satisfaction stats or testimonials from similar customer segments.
- Use success stories tied to specific purchase categories.

Text Advertising (SMS/MMS)

Best Used When:

- Sharing urgent offers on mobile devices with opt-in audiences who already trust you.
- Reinforcing the decision with timely proof.

Avoid When:

- Target audience hasn't explicitly opted in.
- Message lacks urgency or relevance.

Strengths:

- High open rates, immediate delivery.
- Great for "final nudge" conversions.

Weaknesses:

- Strict compliance rules.
- Intrusive if misused.

Common Pitfalls:

- Overusing texts and eroding trust.
- Using vague offers with no credibility elements.

Strategic Opportunities:

- Include brief proof in the copy.
- Pair with an image/MMS of customer use or testimonials.

Brochure-Style Website

Best Used When:

- Serving as the hub of validation after someone hears of you elsewhere.
- Housing proof elements: testimonials, certifications, awards, and press mentions.

Avoid When:

- Never avoid having a website. Ever. You can do it. And you should.
- Did I mention you should have one? Please. It's not as hard as you think.

Strengths:

- Always-on source of credibility and authority.
- Can layer proof in multiple formats: quotes, case studies, logos.

Weaknesses:

- Without SEO or promotion, it may not be seen.
- Design quality directly impacts perceived credibility.

Common Pitfalls:

- No visible proof on the homepage.
- Using fake-looking or vague testimonials.

Strategic Opportunities:

- Include video testimonials, real customer photos, or review badges above the fold.
- Use third-party trust marks (BBB, industry associations) prominently.

Precision Direct Mail

Best Used When:

- Targeting households with personalized, proof-driven offers.
- Including review quotes, customer counts, or "voted best" accolades in the design.

Avoid When:

- If you are skipping personalization.
- Targeting unqualified lists.

Strengths:

- Tangible proof the customer can hold and reference.
- Works well for high-value purchases that require reassurance.

Weaknesses:

- Higher cost per piece than saturation mail.
- No instant interactivity without digital tie-ins.

Common Pitfalls:

- Wasting valuable real estate on generic imagery instead of proof.
- Not integrating tracking (QR codes, PURLs) to measure response.

Strategic Opportunities:

- Feature local customer photos and quotes prominently.
- Use "limited spots left" or "most popular in your neighborhood" language.

Consideration in Perspective

This part of the consumer journey has so much nuance, following my advice rigidly without sinking into particulars could be more trouble than it is help. In an attempt to fill in some gaps amongst these tactics, there are some points that cover most everything on here that need to be called out separately for maximum value. Here are some powerful and independent thoughts in no particular order.

1. Make sure any place you can be reviewed that you have claimed your free listing. It doesn't matter that people don't go to TripAdvisor to look up your foundation repair business. It matters that you own your free real estate. We'll discuss this at length later, but Google's algorithm monitors the internet looking for the validity of your business as a search result. Among those validations is that your reviews are all claimed and used.

2. Make sure your name, address, and phone number in every listing matches your website to the character. If your website says "Suite 302" but your Google My Business listing says "#302," or you have a phone number for your website but a different one on your listings, search

algorithms will index you lower due to the mismatch because it can't be sure this is the same business. The lower index doesn't necessarily mean lower page rankings, but if it does, and it's within your power to manage that, you should do it.

3. Speaking of power to manage, if you worry about having to manage that many listing and review sites, there are inexpensive services out there that can do it for you relatively inexpensively for the value. These services even monitor and respond to reviews for you at whatever level you would like. From basic responses to intricate detail with your approval and influence, you can throttle the workload for yourself with this kind of reputation management service.

4. When it comes to organic social media, keep your expectations extremely low on the engagement metrics telling you anything about the health of your business or a campaign. A critical misstep is to put your social media manager under pressure to translate posts to sales when consideration media is still more heavily influencing readiness than actual sales. Low numbers of likes, shares, comments, etc. are not the important metrics to follow. What's important is that the promises you made in awareness are reinforced and validating in your social channels. People aren't looking for dynamic pages of entertainment necessarily. They are looking for proof.

5. Depending on the consideration phase alone is like having good ground, water, and sunlight without actually planting a seed. Some stuff will grow there, but the harvest won't

necessarily be what you are looking for. Make sure you are not too heavily dependent on consideration options to be your entire funnel just because there are good elements of it that can function like Awareness and Intent can.

Think It Through

* What areas listed here have you not taken advantage of to extend the conversation with potential customers that you will do so now?

* How has your perception of the consideration phase changed from this chapter's information?

* What level of dependence have you forced on this phase to perform like it's a funnel of its own? What ways can you branch out from here?

Chapter 10

THE TUSH PUSH OF INTENT

Aiding the Runner

You're at the goal line. It's 4th down. You need the six points to regain the lead. You and your team get set, and when the ball is hiked to you as quarterback, instead of handing it off, you barrel forward behind your linemen and get a little help from the running back behind you by way of a hard shove and driving legs. In one full motion, the entire line, including the player behind you, gets that last couple of feet you needed to convert the play. Would you believe that this play has been illegal longer than it has been legal?

Before 2004, helping a ball carrier by way of a push or a pull was banished. Since then, it's been perfectly legal because it's incredibly difficult to enforce and there aren't a lot of documented injuries we can pin on it like originally thought. By 2022, it had become so normal a play in short yardage situations that the Philadelphia Eagles popularized it as the "Tush Push" or "Brotherly Shove," helping quarterback Jalen Hurts score several touchdowns on their way to two Super Bowl appearances and even a win.

No Small Feat

Let's put this phenomenon into perspective. The most rushing touchdowns in NFL history from one yard or less is 56 by Marcus Allen. John Riggins had 52, and Emmitt Smith had 47. For those who are not big football fans or history buffs, all three of these men were hired to carry the ball specifically, and did so before 2004 when the rules changed in favor of the infamous shoving. But the odds that a running back or fullback would still have the highest marks in this area is likely. That's why it's so amazing that a quarterback like Jalen Hurts, whose main job is to hand off or throw the ball, is having such success from the goal line.

He's not a running back, and he's only played about a third of the games that these top players in this category have played. However, Hurts is on pace to score 88 times or so from the Tush Push if his career lasts as long and the play stays legal. Proposals to ban it have failed, but that doesn't mean teams won't try to push a little from behind the scenes to make it illegal again. For now, aiding a runner is legal, and more teams will try to exploit the options.

And here I want to draw your attention to two important associations in this real-life metaphor for what Intent Media is, and a third association to help you frame your mind for what you will learn in this chapter. First, intent media functions as a set of plays at the goal line of the consumer journey to get past any last defenses of the mind if the heart hasn't done its job by way of proper awareness and social proof using messages that matter to your customer. The second is that there are important battles to outlaw certain plays by certain players from having the advantage that play and that player offers. We'll speak in detail about this as well. And finally, there is a mistake in thinking about Intent Media that football play callers would never make and yet it gets made thousands of times a day in marketing by advertisers all over the country.

Terrible Play Calling

Let's start with that third association for framing the Tush Push metaphor and work our way backwards. It's the hard part to deal with, so if we get it out of the way, we can concentrate on the "now what" proper usage of Intent Media.

It's not hard to imagine being the play caller for a pro football team that uses this play as well as the Eagles and Jalen Hurts uses it. Here are your facts about using this play:

- On goal line plays, the 'Push works 88% of the time despite being one of dozens on your play sheet, this play accounts for 20% of your scoring.
- You even have situations not at the goal line that help get a first down using it on short yardage plays, keeping your team on the field 76% of the time.

What if someone in the stands yells to you while you are on the sidelines mid-game, "Run the Tush Push every play! It's got all the best stats!" They must be joking, right? Who would ever do that? Marketers. Marketers do that. And it's ruining their business. They just don't all see it yet, and they certainly aren't as public with their negative consequences in this area if they DO see it. But I shine light in dark spaces, so let's walk through this simple truth to say but difficult to put in practice:

Putting too much attention and budget to the end of the funnel tactics and products will hurt your business.

Numbers Do Lie

What would happen if Jalen and crew only ran that one play every time? Initially, the scoring percentage would go down drastically because what makes it work is the short yardage scenarios, not that it scores a lot. If you chase that metric as a marketing play caller without looking at what else affects the outcomes and what scenarios apply, your other numbers related to sales or margins or both with be affected.

Too many marketers don't pay attention to other numbers or related information because the big numbers are propped up by headlines and a bunch of short-term conversions. They are real numbers, important numbers even, but not the only ones that matter to making the decision. A smart offensive coordinator knows better than to listen to advice from the stands, and the smart marketer knows better than to just take the headlines and partial numbers to make a great marketing plan.

The smart coordinator looks at other information to make great decisions. For instance, how effective would my team be without the great offensive line clearing the way? How important are the other 99 yards we put behind us on the field to even get here? Surely there was a great kick return and a healthy combination of tactics and players that kept the defenses of the mind from putting a stop to it wasn't there?

Removing Advantages

The marketing world changes fast, but at the time of this writing, Google in particular is embroiled in an anti-trust law controversy regarding their potential monopoly as a search engine. We can discuss this endlessly, but suffice it to say, even if they are the best in the world at it for a reason, there are people who want the advantage it has to be removed. There is reason to believe that Google is both strong-arming some folks in order to make it the default search engine on some devices and platforms, but at the same time other devices with other search engines as default find people on those platforms searching for Google there to use that platform instead. Perhaps they got carried away with the brotherly shove, but Google scores a lot for businesses for a reason. And it is because of this, much of what we are going to talk about at this stage centers on Google. At least for now, it's a great scoring play at the goal line, perhaps the greatest goal-scoring play, and for this reason alone, you should take it very seriously.

Head vs. Heart

I mentioned earlier that the defenses of the mind are still in play at the goal line. The head operates rationally in your future customers, but it is only necessary to speak to them with logic and reason at the end of the journey when the heart hasn't already let you score from much further back in the funnel. Too many marketers use language like, "Don't forget we also do A/C work," to speak to the mind when speaking to the heart says, "Your A/C owes you rent, let us help you make it pay."

But at the end of the journey, if you haven't built belief in a promise they care about, you have one play or small set of plays that work, and they regularly have to be driven by a logic-oriented decision making, and that's most typically about price. The great news is that if you have done enough in the previous plays of awareness and consideration, you won't have to depend as much on price. You can use it as the play it was designed for, that extra push, and not the only way to score. With that as your framing, these are your best options for converting people at the moment of decision.

PPC / SEM (Pay-Per-Click Search Engine Marketing). Ads displayed in search results when users type relevant keywords.

Paid placement ensures visibility at the highest probability it is the moment of intent.

Best When:

1. You need to capture demand from people actively searching for your exact product/service in the moment they need it. Perfect for urgent needs (HVAC repair, towing, same-day service).
2. Your Search Engine Optimization has not yet helped you reach the first page of the Search Engine Results Page (SERP). Since getting onto page 1 in many markets and various industries is difficult, PPC ensures you can get visibility while you work at that process, which takes considerable time and effort.

Avoid When:

1. Your product requires heavy education before purchase, as it is highly unlikely a prospect would use search when so much is done to prepare them before the search process.
2. You are not budgeted to outbid major players on the most important keywords. If you are a challenger brand, your strategy must be nimble and precise, not a juggernaut of keywords.

Strengths:

- Highly measurable, immediate lead generation.
- Flexible budget control.

Weaknesses:

- Competitive keywords can be expensive.
- Constant changes to Google's algorithm require that it is actively and regularly managed.

Pitfalls:

- Paying for irrelevant clicks due to poor keyword match settings or bad ad copy.
- Assuming more budget needs to be placed on ads vs. SEO strategy.

Opportunities:

- Combine with remarketing to recapture non-converting visitors.
- Since impressions are free, you can use it as its own awareness within the intent end of the funnel.

Role Play:

Riley – With limited budget, she'll likely need to get very specific as to the keywords she buys if she buys at all. If research proves there is particular set of keywords that are highly searched locally, or if she wants to make sure her bank shows up at the top when they type the bank's name, Riley might want to devote that cash to that. Ad copy that talks about competitive rates is critical, because if other media has not made the difference on brand belief, offering a great deal is all she has left to convert.

Chris – Some prospects still won't know or recall that Chris's furniture store is devoted to luxury brands. If any major regional chains are buying those keywords and Chris's store is not likely ranking organically yet, buying the luxury brand's keywords might be a great option. Temporarily at least, up to 40% of budget can be devoted to this to compete until the SEO gets them first page status.

Vanessa – Having a full repair service department available 24/7, Vanessa can put all her effort into acquiring leads that the emergencies homeowners deal with related to HVAC. And since she is likely buying a lot of awareness and consideration media, she can gather intent budget into the times of year more emergencies take place and perhaps build a better focus on those "last-yardage" conversions.

SEO (Search Engine Optimization). The process of improving website visibility in organic (non-paid) search results through content, structure, and authority building.

Best When:

1. You want sustainable visibility that is always "on" for high-intent searches without paying per click.
2. You have a local service area and niche expertise for keywords that are highly searched terms.

Avoid When:

1. You need instant results, as optimizing for search engines takes months, even more than a year in some situations, to improve rankings enough.
2. There is not a lot of competition in your field locally. A brochure website that has enough relevant keywords in it will likely get and keep a decent SERP ranking.

Strengths:

- Builds authority, credibility, and organic lead flow over time.
- Forces discipline in other marketing transformation, as not having other online media aligned works against the strategy.

Weaknesses:

- Slow to build results.
- Requires ongoing technical/content work, as algorithm changes can impact rankings.

Pitfalls:

- Focusing only on broad keywords instead of intent-rich local terms.
- Because it is not "set it and forget it," pay attention to the competitive environment to determine where to alter or update the strategy.

Opportunities:

- Use content to answer high-intent questions, rank for "near me" searches, and leverage your Google My Business Profile.

Role Play:

Riley – With a strong keyword-rich ranking already, Riley's biggest opportunity is to keep developing new content on the website that highlights the value offered to the transactional buyer without making it look inconsistent with the other messaging. Ensuring the communities her bank serves are also well-documented and signaled in the keywords will have a beneficial effect even hyper-locally.

Chris – Having his work cut out for him on the luxury lines, being new to his website, Chris must concentrate on getting the website and all focused media to become the first name in these terms so that over the next 12 to 18 months, he can scale back the PPC in favor of the more engaged organic clicks. Linking articles and press releases about their store's upgrade will definitely support the effort.

Vanessa – being larger, but still a challenger brand, her HVAC company must create more keyword richness by geographic center so that she is in the first seven listings on the SERP. Concentrating on each municipality in the market, starting with those closest to their home base and continuing out to where other media is being placed will actually help organic results where it's most important right now.

CTV / Streaming / OTT. Video ads shown on streaming platforms and smart TVs, targeting audiences based on data on a one to one basis rather than broad broadcast or cable zones that deal with the masses.

Best When:

1. You can deliver video ads directly to targeted households already in-market, using data to match to buying signals. Many TV providers locally can also acquire ads through this delivery method, and coupled at times with their own first party data as well as third party data, the possibilities of reaching your exact target improve a great deal.
2. You can adapt your messaging to fit the short-term conversion without abandoning the long-term messaging strategy. To the consumer, it's all TV, but you know the difference the message can have when you are speaking to a more likely buyer than the masses.

Avoid When:

1. You don't have quality video creative that can make an emotional impact quickly.
2. Your vendors cannot provide you with enough reporting on delivery and other activity to validate the much larger investment.

Strengths:

- Hyper-targeting by household, measurable impressions.
- Blends awareness with intent.

Weaknesses:

- Higher CPMs than broad TV.
- As a newer technology, frequency issues arise (too much on one platform, too few on others).

Pitfalls:

- Treating CTV like traditional TV without using its targeting or retargeting capabilities.
- Not altering thinking from spots like traditional TV with unknown audience sizes to the one-to-one basis of the CTV ad.

Opportunities:

- Pair with search retargeting to show ads to households that recently searched for your product.
- Utilize a third-party service that reports on the alignment of website visits and sales from households that you served ads.

Role Play:

Riley – Depending on whether the sample audience is too small, Riley can use one of her TV vendors to reach an extremely specific type of household based on all kinds of distinctions. If it is indeed too small, she can open geography or remove some peripheral distinctions but still get a highly matched target audience for banking comparatively to other TV options.

Chris – Spreading through the market's whole geography, Chris can utilize streaming options to reach specific households that are of a certain income level rather than just a specific neighborhood. If he has additional knowledge of their likely customers, streaming options might be able to incorporate those into his streaming plan with the luxury brand message.

Vanessa – If she has certain times of year to add TV ads for generators and knows the types of homes to market to, Vanessa can use streaming options to reach those households with that exact message with a specific price point that will get them to call. And using a third-party service, she can match the homes that were served ads this way to calls, form fills, website visits, and sales to gauge success.

Other Intent Options. Use each of these as a means of hyper-focusing on short-term tactics that speak to that final push to convert a customer who is still unsure of the right move. Done well, you can provide the best probability that the rest of the media was worth getting you to this point. Done poorly, it will begin a doom loop of sorts that is difficult to get out of the habit.

Display Ads (Geo-Fenced)

While it is the same format as online billboards, these are served to people in specific geographic zones (like competitor locations or event spaces) while they are using mobile or desktop devices; this is done by way of a virtual polygon drawn around an area, and ads are served to devices that have been inside that polygon during a specific previous time period.

Best When:
You can target people in very specific locations (competitor stores, event venues, neighborhoods) and then follow them online.

Avoid When:
Your target audience isn't concentrated in specific, trackable places.

Strengths:
Pinpoint targeting, measurable foot traffic lift, supports conquesting strategies.

Weaknesses:
Banner blindness, small creative space limits storytelling, and typically cannot stand alone digitally.

Pitfalls:
Wasting impressions on people who were in the polygon but not buyers.

Opportunities:

Use event-based targeting—serve ads to people attending a home show, festival, or sports event in your service area.

Website Chat Bots

Best When:

You want to instantly capture and qualify leads 24/7, especially for high-consideration services where questions are common.

Avoid When:

You can't respond to leads quickly, as automation alone won't close sales.

Strengths:

Increases lead conversion from existing traffic, can pre-qualify and schedule appointments.

Weaknesses:

Poorly scripted bots frustrate users, and bad user experiences can hurt trust quickly.

Pitfalls:

Failing to make hand-off to a real human when needed.

Opportunities:

Integrate with CRM for instant follow-up as well as use bots to promote financing offers or limited-time deals.

E-Commerce Websites

Best When:
You sell products that can be purchased directly without a sales call, or you can take deposits for service bookings online.

Avoid When:
Your offering requires complex quoting or in-person visits before a sale.

Strengths:
Always open, scalable, removes sales friction, and can integrate upsells/cross-sells.

Weaknesses:
Competitive pricing pressure, shipping/logistics challenges for physical goods.

Pitfalls:
Clunky checkout experience causing cart abandonment.

Opportunities:
Use abandoned cart retargeting, bundle products/services for higher order value.

Aggregators (General/Industry-specific)

Best When:
You want quick access to in-market buyers who are comparison shopping (Think: HomeAdvisor, Yelp, or Angie's List, depending on industry).

Avoid When:

You rely on brand loyalty or high margins because aggregators commoditize pricing.

Strengths:

Built-in traffic due to buyers already looking to purchase soon.

Weaknesses:

High competition side-by-side with competitors, lead quality can vary.

Pitfalls:

Not following up instantly; aggregator leads go cold fast because one lead could be presented to several advertisers, and the first to answer wins many times.

Opportunities:

Use as a supplement, not replacement, for owned lead sources; upsell leads to higher-margin products/services once you acquire them to increase lifetime value.

Intent in Perspective

If you took a trip to South Central Colorado and headed west of I-25, you'd find a total gem in the San Isabel National Forest. There are tons of amazing views and trails to get to various peaks, as well as sites to see along the way. It's an incredible place to hike. As I conclude this chapter, let me bring it home with insights on one of my favorite hikes.

Along Highway 165, just past Bishop Castle (an unbelievable hand-made structure with an incredible story of one man's ingenuity) there's an unremarkable road around a turn that takes you up into the mountains about 10 miles or so to a parking area for the trail head for the very remarkable St. Charles Peak. From there, you can hike to the peak in about an hour, stretching roughly two miles upward. There are other ways to get there, but none of it as simple and easy as this for the novice to mildly-trained hiker.

When you get to see the peak and off the trail for the final bear crawl-like climb, it's rigorous, and you need to be in decent shape to complete that last bit of elevation. Due to the thinner air, your heart pounds harder, and your backpack will feel like you've added some large stones along the way. But when you get there, just like with many peaks, you will feel like you are on top of the world. That the grind will have been worth it.

The metaphor I've switched to again, which I promised I'd do to you in the introduction, is that most advertisers don't make the entire climb from the bottom of that mountain. They have to start at the parking lot at the secondary trail head for that last couple of miles for a myriad of reasons. Perhaps they are just starting out and have not scaled enough yet to afford some of those seemingly much larger options in the purchase funnel; perhaps the people who sell some of the larger options have not considered that there are some solutions that can get you enough coverage in the full funnel without breaking the bank; perhaps they just like the benefit of seeing the mountaintop in photos and are comfortable with the smaller feelings of amazing without having the high-stakes risk of the rigor that comes with the journey.

As the zenith of the customer journey, there's a lot of reason to believe and understand its power to convert customers. It puts points on the scoreboard that you can attribute results. It also makes the struggle to get to the peak worth it. Anyone who has ever hiked any mountain to the top knows the feeling and sense of grandeur that any struggle upward returns to you. And that person or business who struggled knows how much better it is to have gotten there in person with their own senses taking it all in. Words can't describe the pay-off properly.

My mixed metaphors of goal-line plays and mountain top experiences may seem like I'm down on Intent Media. I promise you I am not. I just care about the over-indexing businesses do on this part of the funnel, and I want to recalibrate that because it's necessary to offer an alternative way than the often frenetically paced and increasingly fluctuating results that Intent Media offers you. Your growth and scale as a business depends on it. If you want growth, the higher stakes of the other parts of the funnel can make a pay-off so huge that this part of the funnel gets a lot easier to manage at least, or at best, keeps you calm amidst chaos and singularly focused on growing belief in the 95% of the market not yet ready to buy from you.

This may beg the question from you, "so Tom, how do you suggest we recalibrate?" And it is indeed the right question. We'll get to that soon, but before I do, I want to validate Intent Media by sharing one more step after the leads complete their first journey, sale or no sale, through the second chances of Loyalty.

Think It Through

* Have you found frustration with the fluctuating results with PPC and SEO? Has the cost per click and cost per lead risen for the same budget?

* What ways have you convinced yourself that this stage or extremely close to it is all you can afford?

* How well does your ad copy in this space work at the final push to convert a customer?

Chapter 11

THE LIT MATCH OF LOYALTY

L et's take a trip of another kind. Rather than up a mountain, let's get in a make-believe time machine and go back to the public launch date of a well-known company in November of 2011. From its humble Chicago beginnings in October of 2008 to a $12.7 billion valuation and internationally driven revenue just three years later, Groupon was touted as an amazing start-up success. Article after article praised its sky-rocketing value, which included a refusal to sell to Google, who had offered $6 billion previously to own the revenue starlet. But what is Groupon, or perhaps more properly asked, what WAS Groupon, and how does this pertain to Loyalty Media?

For those newer to marketing or perhaps not into the dynamics of the rapid changes occurring in the early 2000s, Groupon formed as a way to help group buying volume to produce better pricing. If enough people would opt into a deal on Groupon, the offer would go live and the group would have access to it. The first deals typically went like this: a pizza place would offer two pizzas for the price of one. If enough of the potential buyers opted into that coupon, the offer was sent to them to redeem. The pizza place would immediately have new customers, filling the purchase funnel and forcing leads through automatically. And the deal was a big hit. As Groupon found success, they expanded to all kinds of verticals...spa services, fitness, travel and experiences, and entertainment. Then professional services were added to the deal and local advertisers had an instant change to the game of Lead-Gen Plinko, one that could streamline the journey down to the most electric parts of the pathway, a great temporary offer. This short-term tactic energized everyday local businesses, and Groupon expanded to dozens of countries by the time it went public in 2011.

Fast forward in our makeshift DeLorean to 2016. Revenue that year hit $3 billion worldwide. Headlines continued to make Groupon the success story to emulate. But deep beneath the surface was a problem few talked about until it was too late, but it is important to discuss so there is proper depth and backdrop to the scene of this chapter. Groupon's downfall saw revenue deplete dramatically for three straight years until the pandemic-led shutdown of in-person services, experiences, and goods virtually obliterated them from the local map. What once was the golden child of lead generation was now a shell of its former self, sparking debates around the world about what happened to such a shooting star. So, what happened?

In addition to the aforementioned pandemic, which really severed the last rope of hope, there were other small factors that could have been corrected but weren't. But those aren't the main reason Groupon tumbled; those only accelerated the demise. Groupon's problem was at the very core of the deal lived an incorrect assumption about human beings and our motivations. Let me explain how their deals worked in better detail first.

The basic economics of the deal were this: your business would make an offer to the opted-in fanbase of Groupon. Your offer, let's say, was for $100 worth of goods that you marked down to $50 for this special deal. But that wasn't your takeaway. For giving you access to their subscribers, Groupon would take just $25 of that $50, making the business's offer actually a quarter of its value returned in revenue. You were effectively selling $100 worth of goods for $25 paid to you by the customer.

In addition to the fact that this deep discount isn't good for the balance sheet, the customer didn't feel the 75% off. It was 50% off because Groupon was taking that $25. This in and of itself isn't the insidious part. What hurt the strategy long-term is that Groupon had a flaw in the psychology of the deal, turning themselves over time into one of the largest cautionary tales in consumer journey history.

The flaw? Groupon believed and taught their advertisers that if Groupon could get them in the door on a deal, the business could upsell them, resell them, or otherwise build a relationship based on that connection. And on the surface, it sounds perfectly reasonable. We'll go into greater detail on what to do about this in a later chapter, but it's important to highlight here the reality that short-term tactics are only a recent phenomenon in the history of marketing, and for millennia, people sold things to each other by way of consistent trust and scarcity of options. With our documented revelation in this book that both of these things have changed, the need to have or perhaps better said, the result of having low immediate trust and more options than you can possibly need has created a place for a medium or even a whole section of the path to purchase specifically designed to support this phenomenon and potentially remove or mitigate the results of the flaw that short-term tactics can create a long-term trust. As I said, more on that later. For now, let's concentrate on what Loyalty Media is, while maintaining this Groupon story as a foundational piece of understanding what it is and why it is important.

Because of the ubiquity of options and the lack of immediate trust, leads fall out of the funnel a lot at the very end; additionally, because so many companies have multiple lines of business, even leads that close have the opportunity to be sold on something else with the same company. These are the two reasons Loyalty Media exists, and it is important to point out that none of them existed before the internet expanded our horizons on options and cynicism. There was no need for this part of the funnel until then.

While you wait a little longer for us to discuss long and short-term tactics and balance, let's look at what the dominant ways businesses use Loyalty Media to upsell or put leads back into the funnel at the consideration phase to move them through to another chance to close them. Before we do though, one more important point related to the messaging and the promise you are delivering in this space: arguably, loyalty has ALWAYS been conditional. Some might argue with me on this, but I can always find at its core a lack of options for taking trust of the customer away.

The three aspects that customers look at when it comes to building loyalty around you and your offer is whether it is good, fast, and inexpensive comparatively, and what combination of these things best fits the need at the time. Any business that can be enough of or all three of these at the same time wins. This is a fundamental reason why Amazon hasn't faded while companies like Groupon failed. Groupon made the good, fast, and cheap unsustainable, while companies like Amazon has good product options, decently fast in delivery, and has a rigorous strategy on pricing models, where prices are set for advertisers to not have to discount so much, but the internet is likely not going to find it cheaper somewhere else for long.

And before we take a look at the Loyalty Media options, I need to underscore "switching costs" as part of your plan for these mediums. Switching costs is the mental leap a consumer has to make to commit to switching to you from one of your competitors. The perceived barrier of friction to make the leap is real if they believe it, and your offer is going to have to overcome it by way of price considerations or some other reduction in mental cost for the same money.

An example of this is my penchant for hanging on to an older model smartphone for too long. I'm not the world's worst, but I have friction to adopt new tech in these cases because I think about the time spent in a retail store making the switch, the time it will likely take to download or reclaim apps, and all kinds of things that aren't always real issues. Apple has to work overtime in building loyalty to the new tech, but the barriers to switch to Android are even higher. I'm sure we all have immediate situations much like mine that remind you that switching costs are an important factor when buying Loyalty Media. Most of the time, it's about price, but reduction of other losses is just as valuable sometimes. Think of this when it comes to your messaging, and let's get started.

Display Ad Retargeting. Online billboards are served specifically to people who have already interacted with your website, app, or other digital assets while they are on the internet doing something else like checking scores, reading articles, or otherwise looking at internet-delivered content.

When to use:
You want to keep your brand top-of-mind after site visits, abandoned carts (if you also sell via e-commerce website), or any other content interactions.

When not to use:

If your creative is generic and doesn't reflect the customer's past behavior or needs, these ads will be ignored.

Strengths:

Display retargeted keeps your brand visible post-visit and is likely an efficient use of ad dollars since the audience is pre-qualified.

Weaknesses:

It can be annoying if frequency isn't managed and ad fatigue sets in quickly if the consumer has already made a different decision since considering you.

Pitfalls:

You can hurt your brand with over-exposure, failing to exclude converted consumers, and stale creative that ignores context of their interaction with you.

Opportunities:

You can segment by user behavior (cart abandoners, product viewers), use sequential messaging to nurture, and tailor creative to reinforce purchase confidence.

Role Play:

Riley – If the website page the potential customer visits explores auto loans, Riley might have an option to have an auto-loan specific display ad delivered to that user, perhaps with some more information that could tip the scale in their favor. Or if the user is already a known customer, serving a display ad about a customer-only event may be an option.

Chris – Since the website has an e-commerce function, Chris can use display ads to retarget consumers who have put a luxury item in a cart but clicked away without buying. Putting the actual item in the ad with a call to action might get that consumer to return to finish their purchase.

Vanessa – Perhaps a user has looked at the page on Vanessa's website related to various brands of A/C units they carry during late spring. Leading into the summer months, she might do well to serve that same user display ads about system checks with a current special or the offer of a free inspection. In each of these cases, the display ads have links that, if clicked, send the user to the correct page for conversion.

Email Nurturing (CRM). This is based on an internally driven, automated or semi-automated email sequencing delivered to existing customers or leads, aimed at relationship-building, cross-sell/upsell, or retention.

When to use:

Creating deeper connection, database emails can be utilized for onboarding or activation, post-purchase follow-up, renewal reminders, or personalized offers.

When not to use:
If your email list is unsegmented or you lack quality content beyond promotions, this will annoy prospects or potential repeat and upsell customers.

Strengths:
It's direct, personal, cost-effective, measurable, scalable, and permission-based.

Weaknesses:
Proper utilization requires strong list "hygiene" and strategy and inbox clutter reduces attention.

Pitfalls:
You can hurt the brand by over-emailing, ignoring personalization, or poor mobile formatting.

Opportunities:

- Segment emails by lifecycle stage.
- Incorporate behavioral triggers (open, click, purchase).
- Test subject lines and CTAs to maximize engagement.

Role Play:

Riley – With a CRM tool that carries a robust segmentation feature, Riley can custom-build emails speaking to specific actions she wants previous customers to take. Perhaps those who are of a certain life stage, just took out a loan, or just opened a checking account for their student, would all have tailored emails to remind, offer, or educate.

Chris – Despite the database being previous customers with no sense of who would buy luxury lines or not, Chris can create buzz to former buyers that his furniture is getting an upgrade and is passing that upgrade along to them. An invitation to a kick-off event would perhaps make this feature do something special to indicate and initiate the changes at the store. Removing those who already RSVP'd he can automate a sequenced drip of emails making previous customers feel valued to return.

Vanessa – Using her CRM Service Titan, Vanessa can set reminders for filter changes, timing for service, or give valuable insights on conserving energy in the home. As a non-sales solicitation, the call to action creates deeper connections with customers who have had her company install, or create better bonds with an even different email for those who have just had a service done.

Social Retargeting / Search Retargeting. Ads are delivered to social platforms or SERPs respectively targeting users who previously visited your site, interacted with your content, or searched for relevant terms.

When to use:

If you want to re-engage warm audiences on the channels where they spend time daily or have shown active interest with relevant keywords, ads can be delivered in several methods, including display, social ad unit, or video.

When not to use:
You'll find difficulty getting results if audience size is too small due to no scale or the creative doesn't vary from prospecting-focused ads.

Strengths:
Social and search have high visibility where users are proven to be active, with strong targeting precision, and the opportunity to reinforce brand loyalty.

Weaknesses:
The cost to reach a customer that close to the sale is high, especially when audiences are too small, and it requires an ongoing creative refresh to ensure high validity.

Pitfalls:
Repetition without relevance wastes money and frustrates prospects, steering them somewhere else.

Opportunities:
Show loyalty rewards, highlight community or the brand story, and use dynamic product or service ads tied to past views.

Role Play:

Riley – Using current opportunities provided by bank management, Riley can set a plan to run display ads to households in which various HELOC terms have been used in search engines. Knowing that a prospect is investigating home equity options opens up creative options to serve ads too those households based on that behavior and increase the likelihood of getting a new customer by way of a loan for an upgrade to their home.

Chris – The luxury lines being so specific, anyone searching brand or product keywords could be served all kinds of offers and communications tailored to fit the strong probability that this could be a loyal customer of the store one day.

Vanessa – Running two separate campaigns, Vanessa can target those who have searched with terms describing issues with their A/C unit with a repair special ad, and at the same time run a change-out offer to those who have searched specific brands of units. Custom retargeting campaigns means each prospect is more likely to get a valid ad for the respective issue.

Experience Marketing. Real-world or virtual experiences designed to deepen customer relationships such as events, workshops, community gatherings, VIP clubs, or immersive brand interactions.

When to use:
You may have a desire to reward loyal customers, create memorable brand touchpoints, or build community around your brand. This affords that while not hard selling what's already been sold.

When not to use:

If execution is half-hearted, underfunded, or disconnected from your core customer base, it could have an opposite than desired effect.

Strengths:

When used as true connection, it builds emotional loyalty, strong word-of-mouth potential, and deepens brand attachment.

Weaknesses:

It's harder to scale because it requires strong planning and budget, and ROI is indirect and not immediately measurable.

Pitfalls:

Avoid sloppy execution, prevent low attendance, and clearly tie the experience to business objectives.

Opportunities:

Create tiered experiences for loyalty levels, integrate digital/social media amplification (photos, livestreams), partner with complementary brands.

Role Play:

Riley – Partnering with a local car dealership, Riley could run a promotion with a huge event for all student customers in which a new car is awarded to honor roll students by way of a drawing. The event could tie in other vendors who would help offset the costs by way of a booth at the event and even smaller giveaways for those who did not win the car. Using social to promote it ahead of time and utilizing press by inviting them to cover the event could stretch value considerably.

Chris – Using a local summer series of movies in the park held by his town, Chris could set up a booth to collect prospects by way of registering to win the "Best Seat in the House", a virtual living room set up in a prominent spot where a family can upgrade from a blanket on the grounds to luxury seating accompanied by snacks and drinks in front of the movie screen. The build-up to the winner being announced just before showtime ensures everyone at the event knows you and what you offer in a fun setting.

Vanessa – At holiday events hosted by a local charity, one for Independence Day and one for Christmas, Vanessa can set up a virtual tent passing out gourmet hot chocolate in the winter and cold drink options in the summer. The opportunity is to both align with the values of the charity as well as become synonymous with comfort based on providing warmth in the winter and cool refreshment in the summer.

Direct Mail (1:1). Highly personalized physical mail sent to existing customers, often with offers, reminders, or thank-you messages.

When to use:
You want to create a tangible touchpoint in a digital-heavy world, especially for high-value customers or subscription renewals.

When not to use:
If personalization is weak or customer value doesn't justify cost, it could backfire.

Strengths:
Being so tangible, it's harder to ignore than digital options like email, and it has strong impact the more personalized it is. This makes it good for differentiation to a select group of important referral partners, distributors, and friends of the business by value.

Weaknesses:
The cost per piece to send is likely high, it is slower to deploy, and dependent on good data quality.

Pitfalls:
Generic creative would be counterproductive, sending to outdated addresses would lose the high-value touch, and failing to track results doesn't help galvanize the value.

Opportunities:
Handwritten notes, VIP gifts, and integrating QR codes or personalized URLs to bridge offline and online engagement.

Role Play:

Riley – Due to banking regulations, the bank is excluded from giving gifts to people of certain kinds of accounts. With this limitation, Riley chooses to have the team write hand-written thank you notes on company letterhead to its best wealth management clients also indicating a small donation was made in their name to a local charity.

Chris – As a means of indicating a touch of class, Chris sends a small gift basket from Harry & David to all the biggest customers to thank them for their business.

Vanessa – Returning to all new market builds that did not redeem the offer placed on the units in the attic when built, Vanessa and her team can send a note to the new homeowners whose names they don't yet know. However, they can share the offer to direct them again or print the unique QR code that is on their unit where the discount offer for the maintenance plan is placed.

Loyalty in Perspective

By now, you should be able to see that Loyalty Media options are an amazing paradox of the lit match of short-term advertising that burns out and goes cold if not accompanied by other sustainable materials that create much larger sales fires. It must be attached to other strategies and tactics. Longer-term, heart-focused pursuit of customer beliefs about the product or service you offer is the extremely flammable material that needs the short-term, logic-focused lit fuse whose only issue is timing of the burn to the conversion point. Your aim is to pay attention to what combination of flammable materials and ignition capabilities fit together to create the fire you are looking for.

The rest of this book is an attempt to build on what you now know. With this insight, you can better determine the balance of long and short initiatives, both with creative messaging and even the advertising product message delivery choices themselves. This should give you tremendous hope and energy that the tools you have access to locally can be used in a combination that fits your budget and any other bandwidth of time, energy, and other resources.

Think It Through

* What customer data collection methods do you currently use? Are there ways you can upgrade this to create better connections with lost leads or customers who could buy again?

* What does the Groupon story tell you about the way an advertiser must balance long and short-term tactics?

* What historical data, both sales and customer information, can you study to determine trends that might indicate whether your brand's promise has been a short-term financial value or a long-term belief value?

Chapter 12

THE BALANCING ACT

'Dunk in the Dark' Debunked

I first heard of Mark Ritson in February of 2013, when a YouTube video came across my screen showing him verbally skewering lazy journalists and marketing pundits about the success of Oreo for a well-timed tweet during the Super Bowl. For those of you not aware of the reference, Oreo was praised for a viral social media post about their sandwich cookies that alluded to a cultural moment during an accidental blackout in the stadium during Super Bowl XLVII. Ritson, with his blunt, British-rooted wit and charm, highlighted the fact that even a viral social media post couldn't get 1/250th of the reach that an ad in the Super Bowl would have gotten, not to mention the extended reach beyond that if the TV ad was worthy of word of mouth. Additionally, he corrected the thought that this was great marketing at all. It was publicity and buzz, but it didn't drive any noticeable sales for Oreo.

At the time, I loved what he had to say and shared it with my co-workers and team, but for all the wrong reasons. I was in regional management for a large cable and broadband company, and the rise of social media was eating into our TV ad revenue year after year. Mark Ritson had no reason to support my cause or knowledge of it, but he carried the torch with the rest of the story on Oreo's viral tweet. TV's reach, Super Bowl or otherwise, dwarfed any other newfangled ad product's ability to reach prospective customers and convert them into buyers. I strummed that chord any chance I got.

At that same time, while American companies large and small gorged themselves on the reporting available by the shiniest new objects in the history of advertising, Les Binet and Peter Field published "The Long & the Short of It" from across the pond. The noise level in the States from the feasting on click attribution and other tangible metrics from these revolutionary ad products drowned out what I now know to be the solution to the advertising world's problems chasing efficiency with attribution. That research piece will arguably become the greatest chance for marketers all over the world to keep from overcorrecting when something new comes out, but for nearly a decade, only the committed peers of Binet & Field paid close attention to it as more than anecdotal.

Those who made the findings of "The Long & Short of It" their mantra, especially British agencies and large international brands, started realizing what took smaller brands and American companies too long to figure out. The lingering effects of the pandemic accelerated the demise of many local brands, and private equity firms that only know efficiency and attribution metrics are headed for more headwinds. In fact, most of the local marketing public STILL hasn't figured out how to properly implement what these preachers of sound marketing promote, and this is a large part of why I am writing this book.

A Parenthetical Statement Respecting the Greats

I have no illusions of capacity for being the American version of the British-Australian apologist for Binet & Field's work like Mark Ritson does so well. He's smarter than me, more creative, more astute, more educated, and has more experience than I do. However, I have worked with hundreds if not thousands of businesses at the decision maker level in large and small markets all over this country in obscurity for a quarter century, and I know American markets and how various local cultures influence advertising and results. This book is an attempt to give enough of you enough repeatable value from the collection of patterns I have curated into one source.

My lack of international depth, education, and experience aside, I believe I can supply enough of what these giants discern to local advertisers in the U.S., so I'm still going to attempt it. The fact that you have stayed with me so far means you either think I'm crazy and you are planning your scathing critique, or I'm onto something. I've been studying these people and other American leaders of the marketing and advertising industry like Roy H. Williams, Seth Godin, and Jonah Berger for so long, and so in depth, it qualifies me to provide you further insights compiled from them attached to what I've already studied in my own experiences just for you.

To be clear, I didn't invent any of this so far. There's nothing proprietary about my ideas. I've just put in the work and studied patterns of behavior and activity; then I married it to principles that some of the smartest people on the planet have been generous to share or I've paid personally to find out, giving you the maximum effect that I can. But we're turning to a part of the book that I need to make perfectly clear came from someone else or several someone-elses, which I have and will note, so you know who to study next for verification of my credibility to support you, should you still need social proof from me. After all, I have made a promise with my own brand, and the possibility you need other proof to believe me is strong. I'm following my own advice.

Chocolate Chips

If you've come this far, my explanation of the Binet & Field research below shouldn't deter you from studying it in its entirety. It should make you want to search it out like I did. It's fascinating and has multiple applications. However, I need to fuse the value into what I'm supporting you with for context on my assertions, because you can't make chocolate chip cookies and then try to remove the chips when they are out of the oven. This research is fundamental to your local marketing strategic planning and is a mess to extricate, so here is a very basic summary.

Principle 1: The most effective campaigns combine both long-term branding and short-term activations.

Principle 2: The stronger the brand in the heart of the consumer, the more effective short-term initiatives are.

Principle 3: Over-reliance on short-term behaviors reduces margins, while brand building significantly reduces price consciousness.

Principle 4: The overwhelmingly successful campaigns use branding initiatives to sow seed in good ground and use short-term initiatives to harvest the crops.

Principle 5: Balance is required of long and short, and they skew differently based on many factors, but the overall average is 60% brand or long-term and 40% performance or short-term.

It is from here that I want to slow down and help you build your funnel and balance it. Too many marketers see the 60/40 split average and immediately ignore some nuance for their industry required, of which there is plenty. Listed below are the top considerations for balancing long and short initiatives. Occasionally, I'll mention the ad products conducive to the consideration as well, but we'll focus more on the dividing line between them later in this chapter.

Nuance #1: Competitive Landscape Factors

Local markets require much more due diligence than national or international brands because the effect of the dynamics are exaggerated due to large differences. The relatively smaller size of the market means there is a limit to the effects of some good practices; the available resources to study the market aren't as easily accessible, and the competitive environment all play a factor. The local stage requires a tremendous amount of versatility.

Let's take SEO in a small market as an example. If your market is Youngstown, Ohio, and there are only 5 competitive companies besides yours, how much less important is SEO strategy than it would be for the same industry in Columbus, Ohio, where there are 30 competitors? Or how about Cleveland where there are 50? When the first seven listings matter the most, a business in Youngstown can immediately see an opportunity to divert marketing funds to something else unless there is a problem in search results.

Too many local marketers accept the headlines-for-clicks' sake, major brand strategies, or other market nuances and blindly apply them to their marketing strategy. The consequences are potentially devastating because the reality is that you can't adopt a national brand strategy locally, and local brand strategy can't necessarily scale up. They are altogether different, and it's one reason small companies have the hardest time becoming a major national player. What works here doesn't automatically work there, and vice versa.

Nuance #2: Purchase Frequency

Let's say you have a solar power company that installs panels on roofs. What good would any of the Loyalty Media options be for marketing to previous buyers besides getting referrals, perhaps? A homeowner who is now getting solar energy delivered from the panels above doesn't have a second reason to buy. This has to be something you consider when it comes to media options you use, and it will affect your balance of long- and short-term mechanics and messaging. The lower the frequency of purchasing, the heavier the company must depend on brand growth rather than performance marketing.

On the other hand, if you sell hamburgers and have 3 locations in town, the potential for frequency of purchasing is much higher, and therefore can win on the "Tush Push," where activation tips the scales. Concentration on special offers, coupons, etc. plays better into the marketer's playbook. Of course, it doesn't mean brand isn't important. It won't matter the discount or special if the customer has other reasons not to trust you. The balance of long and short for you in this case would likely be the inverse of the solar company.

Nuance #3: Price Point Differences

Using the same analogy from Nuance #2, solar power and hamburgers have much different price points. The mental energy it should take to make a decision about a meal is not as exhausting as deciding whether to put solar panels on the house. While there are some married couples at supper time on a

Thursday who might disagree about mental energy requirements, a tremendous amount of risk exists for not thinking through such a large price point as solar. Depending on the requirements, let's say we're talking about the difference between $15 and $15,000.

The lower the ticket item or service, the more you can calibrate your plan to performance marketing. The higher the overall ticket, the more you should calibrate the balance to growth marketing. And since I repeat this over and over because it will always be important, how you use these items matters as much as the price point differences. Long-term messages need to be about why they should buy from you with emotion; short-term messages must carry a high dose of logic.

Nuance #4: Emotion/Logic Resonance

Speaking of emotion vs. logic, the higher the emotion of the brand's promise, the more the marketing will need to skew to long-term initiatives, messaging, and advertising products. The lower emotion required, the more you should index on short. For instance, let's say a fertility clinic is looking at building an advertising plan. It would be extremely bad form to discuss price points or discounts in those ads because that's not where these families are; they are feeling with their hearts, not thinking with their heads. To advertise to them in any way about prices would disrespect the process they are in. It doesn't mean you can't use pricing to help them make complete choices, but your ads will fail if you don't lead with the heart.

In situations like these, because emotions are so incredibly volatile, most advertisers will recalibrate to a 90/10 or higher balance to avoid frustrating the client. In these cases, it's still not the message that is part of the 10% of short-term, but in the product only. I've only seen one emotionally salient industry mention price one time and it was only one advertiser. "Even our prices show we care" toes the line for a funeral home, and it's easy to cross it for negative effect.

The logic-driven decision-making of pest control, on the other hand, can fall back into short-term strategies for ad product and message because people just have a problem they want to go away quickly and affordably. They won't be thinking about weighing the emotion of anything except about how they feel when they see an infestation of pests or large rodent. No belief systems about the brand's promises will be weighed outside of "can you solve my bug problem."

One caveat to this line of thinking before we move on: you may take my words in each nuance and immediately begin aligning yourself into a simple decision tree of if/then statements about long and short initiatives. But when emotion can be involved in message and ad product, don't dismiss too quickly that your company sells a commodity or a pragmatic service like fixing leaky faucets and is a short-term strategy-driven plan. Some of the world's most famous and enduring brands sell a commodity and use price points. But some of the world's most famous and enduring brands sell a feeling and make it easier to sell a commodity on a higher price point.

When Apple introduced the iPhone in 2007, Microsoft CEO Steve Ballmer dismissed it and claimed the new smartphone would not gain any significant market share. The cost to buy it was much higher and didn't have a stylus or physical keyboard. I can almost hear you giggle at the terrible prediction. Now, before I enshrine Mr. Ballmer into the worst hot-takes hall of shame, let me also say that I and many others didn't know what Steve Jobs and the team at Apple knew was going to happen. If I was as famous at the time, I could have easily gone viral for the wrong reasons, especially if I was the guy supplying systems to all of Apple's competitors and had a lot of bias built into me for that.

But here's the thing. Ballmer and so many other predictors of outcomes that never came true would come to the same conclusion if following my advice about nuance on price points as black and white situations. What pattern I am trying to highlight is that when a brand can take a principled leap into the emotion of a thing as the customer's reason to buy, and remain patient while they wait out the commodity-driven sales of competitors, the overall share will statistically be higher, and the margins will be better. This is a difficult gray area that you must know or have help in finding the emotionally charged reason people will buy your commodity or pragmatic service. In these cases, you will come to realize you aren't selling the commodity at all; you are selling the outcome that commodity provides. Speaking to that will give you another chance to recalibrate your short-term into more of a long-term strategy. So you don't sell the world's latest technological advancement. But do you do things in a way that taps into solving problems the customer cares about? If so, they may not camp out the night before every time you launch something new, but they will throw their money at you.

Nuance #5: Educational Complexity

Simply put, some products and services require a heavy amount of education, and some don't. However, if a company has multiple lines of business, advertising each line should have its own strategy and path to purchase. To explain this, let's imagine a fictitious business in the home services industry, much like Vanessa's in share and growth expectations, but this one has several more lines of business.

Veep Home Services offers HVAC work, including service and change-out, as well as new builds. But Veep also provides electrical and plumbing expertise, and it's not contracted out. Veep has three separate teams in-house, and depending on whether it's commercial or residential, most of those teams are separate in work orders and scope. With recent government regulations taking effect, Veep needs to take special care to tell homeowners what needs to happen if they are going to take advantage of the options with HVAC efficiency standards when replacing their systems. Immediately, the HVAC business-to-consumer space needs a longer-term plan to help potential customers get out in front of it. But because there is still a need to highlight 24/7/365 emergency service if your system goes out in extreme temperatures, Veep will likely use their end-of-funnel ad products to keep that short-term, logic-driven need to acquire customers with urgent needs.

At the same time, electrical and plumbing can utilize a similar strategy, and business-to-business commercial services of all three lines of business should definitely be focused on brand and relationship with contractors who would take advantage of their new build services. To an outsider, it could look like a jumbled mess, but to Veep, it's calculated and aligned with balance in every place. This way, when Generac offers them some co-op ads during extreme temperature times of the year, Veep can incorporate that seamlessly because all it takes a quick study of the balance and a small tweak if necessary to keep the chosen balance in line. Sales numbers and margins will show the business if any temporary changes need to be made and can easily detect when to move back.

Allowing the nuance to keep you flexible if you were Veep means that the long term feeds the short term as they are not working independently. This is also why at some point it doesn't matter how many distinctive short-term ads a car dealer has when they have 17 rooftops. The name will be out there so much, the familiarity might mean the short-term initiatives or price points even articulated on TV won't be remembered as much as the dealer name because it is so much of the available share of auto advertising. But just in case the familiarity isn't there, the dealer will still do the short-term initiatives.

The Human Experience

Whether it's financial services or flower arrangements; roofing or restaurants; pool building or pest control; higher education or urgent care, there are principles to follow and nuance to sink into. The challenge of your work in marketing will be to determine what nuances go into effect within the principles, but that's the fun part if you are in this business. Isn't the challenge of solving a complex problem to make something work better a great value in the human experience? Some people choose engineering, or politics in their attempt to make the world better; marketers choose the art of words and feelings coupled with the science of strategy and data to improve the way we interact with each other.

A Principled Approach

In times of uncertainty, which I suppose is now ironically any day of any month of any year in the modern information age we live, a skeletal format for approaching media and messaging options is in order. There must be a way we can simplify the complexity of it all, and the conclusion to this chapter is your bone structure. Feel free to fill in the muscle tissue, nerve centers, and vital organs to your specifications based on the nuances discussed here.

Awareness

Products: Choose as broad a base as budget allows, whether 60%, 90%, 10%, or something in line with the principles shared here. Ease back on targeting as much as possible because you need as many people talking as possible. Too narrow here and you suffer from too little reach and too little frequency. Find likely unduplicated reach on as many media as possible.

Messaging: Because it can get expensive, keep the message extremely narrow and the concentration on what you want the customer to FEEL. As previously mentioned, various forms of video have the biggest influence on those emotions, so start there. Avoid the trap of trying to tell people everything about you as time is short. Leave something behind the counter than you put out on display so to speak. They will linger later and learn more in Consideration.

Consideration

Products: Here, your targeting options can tighten. You'll pay more for a more validated lead, but coupling them with the Loyalty Media options that follow will keep watering and giving sunlight to the seeds you planted with Awareness.

Messaging: As a consistent and versatile phase, capitalize on the awareness you built by having proof everywhere they can search it online. Where applicable, expect to spend more time with the prospect as they expect in this phase of the journey to linger. Long-form video, articles and whitepapers on the website, and educational information specific to your company are worthy areas of messaging focus.

Intent

Products: Your targets are as tight as can be for the product capability. You'll pay the highest there is for a valid lead comparatively, but the moment of conversion is extremely close, making it worth it. Test and track activity of the prospect with your ads and test, test, test some more with messages.

Messaging: Time-bound, specific offers on the products or services in the highest demand or easiest to convert is key. Your copy in search results based on certain keywords is critical if the prospect is looking for the right business to click from the list. Think about what pain point you are solving in that moment of conversion.

Think It Through

* What ways do you approach media that belies the balance that great marketing minds tell us we ought to have? Are there any initiatives, messages, or products you over-index on?

* What principles do you have the largest opportunity for growth as a marketer and what do you think you ought to do to begin that growth?

* What nuances within the principles of balance have you had the most difficulty with understanding or putting to use for positive effect?

Chapter 13

BEFORE YOU BUY

N ow that we have covered the locally available media options you can buy, the balance of long and short initiatives, and profusely peppered in how important creative is, we have some more digging to do. Another layer of data as you sink into the particulars will help you decide which media to buy when all things appear to be equal. A little-known fact is there are insights in the market that will help with specific vendor options, and many of them are free to you. We'll talk at length about your sales reps soon, and the ways they can or should influence your decisions as a third layer, but here we'll discuss how to use the data all around you, both publicly available and by subscription.

For this exercise, I'm going to assume you already have boundaries set for you if you have a wholesaler or manufacturer agreement or you are otherwise clear on your geographical service area; but for those who do not, understanding the intricacies of your geography is critical for successfully choosing media. For instance, one zip code among forty zip codes might account for 15% of the spending in the market for your industry. You can get that intelligence from a demographic study tool below, but only if you are choosing an area with clear boundaries at the start. Keep in mind that zip codes sometimes bleed into more than one county, school districts follow their own lines, and cities have multiple sets of boundaries sometimes where there is an extra territorial jurisdiction (ETJ). Sometimes it isn't enough just to tell vendors the geography in generalities so they don't inadvertently add to or subtract from areas in which you intend to advertise.

Take a look at the expansive options in this layer, where to go to find them if it isn't obvious, and what you can do with them:

Demographics.

U.S. Census Bureau (census.gov) – Look for population centers as well as anonymized age, income, and household intelligence. If there you are looking to buy billboards, for instance, there's plenty to confirm or retool about various demographics within your footprint to make better choices.

City-Data.com – Publicly available maps reveal all kinds of data on local levels that the Census Bureau might have, plus information about local aspects like infrastructure, schools, medical, and other business details. As a cross-reference to the census data, you can double-check for accuracy or add depth to decisions about your targeting.

Local Government Portals – Many cities have stats by block that could prove useful in some of those short-term tactics. Look to see if a municipality has a public GIS (geographic information system) that typically has mapping and analysis that government officials use to make decisions that could affect your business and how it goes to market.

Economic Environment.

Bureau of Labor Statistics (BLS) – Information about jobs by industry as well as wage information and unemployment stats can give you insights about the market as well as company initiatives that pertain to marketing. Imagine doing recruitment ads that have a better plan based who is employed and for how much, and where they live. Ad copy can have so much more value with these insights.

Local Chamber of Commerce – Besides being a sponsorship opportunity within the business community, so much word of mouth passes through these places. Having membership for sales and marketing that is also actively participating adds color to local decisions for the company and extends the promises made in ads.

Economic Development Corporation – Local EDCs work to attract developers, retailers, builders, and other businesses to your city.

Keeping on the pulse of what happens here can help you plan growth and strategy based on the EDC's new projects and incentives they provide to outsiders looking to invest in town.

Consumer Behavior.

AdMall – Provided to you typically by one or more of your advertising sales reps, AdMall is a treasure trove of data that really requires you to get specific with them about what you want because if you don't, they'll possibly inundate you with too much; perhaps ask for consumer spending and think to ask for specifics about what you might want to know about local customers as a profiling measure. AdMall aggregates and subscribes to a lot of data that goes deeper within many of the sources in this chapter, so it is worth it to ask your reps for specific intelligence.

Review Sites – While you are giving social proofs to potential customers, you can also investigate what the market culture and behavior is like.

Google Trends – Studied by region or metro area, Google has all kinds of free information about product or service demand and signals in the marketplace.

Esri Tapestry – There are plenty of free reports by area on psychographics and lifestyle intelligence you can use to get the pulse of the market.

Advertising Landscape.

Before I share these, understand that not all of your local vendors subscribe to all of these. You will find some have some of these and some have none of these. Obviously, those who bring you value in this intelligence earn some rights to propose that perhaps others don't, but I've never heard of any vendor only providing this for paying customers.

Media Radar/Vivvix – Imagine being able to detect what your local competition or even some out-of-market regional players are spending in your marketplace on several kinds of awareness specific ad products and video-related platforms.

Nielsen AdIntel – Focused more on scaled brands, local advertisers can study strategy and product mix across every major media type spent by an advertiser. Perhaps a local company would like to mirror a plan of a major advertiser in their industry or just get a clear understanding about how their ad dollars are being spent.

Media Monitors – Even more competitive information to drive strategy can be found by way of monitoring broadcast TV, cable, radio, CTV/OTT, display ads and even print platforms in real time.

Spyfu/Semrush – Study all kinds of trends for your industry by looking at what specific competitors are doing with keywords, from short and long tail keywords for SEO as well as keywords and spending for PPC.

Google Ads Transparency Center – If a competitor is buying PPC, but the budget isn't visible in one of the other platforms, you can still use this feature too see the ads, ad volume, and who is buying for that company. It includes the ability to see what ads are showing on all of Google's products, including YouTube.

Facebook Ads Library – Instantly study the ads that are running for any advertiser anywhere. Get ideas on creative elements for your own A/B testing as well as areas of focus in the ads.

This list is prescriptive, but not exhaustive. There may be some more hyper-local or lesser-known tools out there that various vendors of yours have or peers in your industry use. Listen to see if there is more out there, not to replace the values to what I have listed, but to add more sight lines to the plans you build. There's nothing wrong with that, so long as it doesn't give you analysis paralysis. You may find that you can get all you need from AI platforms like Copilot or ChatGPT. At a minimum you can ask for information from your reps by asking the question in a better way. At maximum, you won't need to consult them much and wonder whether the data you receive is accentuating positives and not showing realism about negatives.

I maintain my belief that creating familiarity about solving a problem your customers care about overcomes a massive lack of insight on where that message goes. But because we live in the era we live in, efficiency is still an itch that marketers want to scratch even if it doesn't readily change sales. And since there are clues and proofs that the advertising is working, the next chapter is devoted entirely to what to do to make sure it's working once you've activated a plan.

Think It Through

* Before you consult any vendor and utilize their data, are you using what's free and available to you through local word of mouth channels? What changes to that should you make considering the opportunity?

* What kinds of things would you list as data you would like to know to inform your decisions? Anything from this list you can ask vendors to supply to you?

* Are you someone who can become paralyzed by too much data? What ways can you scale back what you seek so you have enough to know the next right thing to do?

Chapter 14

AFTER YOU BUY ADS

Advertising is based on probabilities, and when efficiency and attribution slowly then rapidly replaced real metrics starting a couple decades ago, we started believing we could do something better with probabilities in something other than proper creative and delivering on the promises made in the creative. The fact that we could trace every action and impression now meant somehow that we knew what was sure about those probabilities. But this false sense of accuracy has put marketers on too many side quests.

If you are going to inspect what you expect out of your advertising, you really need to put some metrics back into your own personal truth teller, so that the picture you get is more complete. To be clear though, you still won't know everything about everything, but you can get a layered look at value in the data, some of which is available online, and the rest of it is internal. Here's a look at the nine most important data metrics that matter to successful brands for evaluating media mixes. These metrics are independent of the distractions caused by outside headlines of the day. Overlaying these metrics will eliminate many of the gaps in knowing whether the marketing is working as intended.

Sales Trends Are Undervalued

1. Month Over Month Gross Sales. This provides an immediate pulse check, especially for short-term sales objectives. If your business is seasonal, look at gross sales for the same month prior year.

2. Quarter over Quarter Gross Sales. This highlights the cyclical nature of the industry if there is any. For instance, new installs for A/C will likely be stronger in Q3 than Q2. New car sales for Q4 will be better than Q1. Converting the view to same quarter prior year like you did the month is critical in these types of business sales cycles when quarter by quarter in the same year gives you the wrong story.

3. Year over Year Gross Sales. This highlights the pace of the full plan against the pace of the previous plan period or accommodates sales cycles, especially for those that have long tails between first calls and closing. Additionally, those who are creating memories and familiarity and have the patience for the long game in an established industry will likely only look at this sales trend or wait to look at a sales trend until they can see this view.

4. **Industry Sales Trends.** How a business compares to the industry if it can be known gives a ton of context for numbers that may not tell the full story in the first three metrics. For instance, if wholesale suppliers are up or down, year over year, you can gauge your pace against the field. For instance, a client who was down 4% year to year during their most important sales period of the year learned that their suppliers were down 22-40% during the same time period. This indicates the client was beating the market and increasing share. When the industry is down, share growth becomes the new metric within this layer. If the industry is up, growth percentage similarity confirms holding of share of the market.

Google Metrics That Matter Most

5. Direct Website Visit Trends. How many times each month have potential customers gone straight to the website by typing out the website name? No direct performance marketing attribution to an ad or even SEO is available in this case, but it can speak to the plan overall. Ads are working when direct traffic goes up and is relatively in line with the increase in sales and ad spend.

6. Organic Website Conversion Trends. How many times did potential customers submit themselves as a lead in the website that was NOT a PPC click to the website? This will give you a true comparison of growth marketing and performance marketing head-to-head. You can tweak the

balance one way or the other based on the results over time or sometimes right away.

7. New Customer Trends. How many customers who have never purchased with your business make a purchase? Eliminating repeat business shows a better driver of funnel filling, not just the loyalty loop, which can inadvertently skew numbers. Additionally, businesses that depend heavily on referrals should give some but not too much credit to the media for aiding word of mouth. This layer has holes in it as a stand-alone metric due to the subjectivity of the attribution, but it is a worthy metric specifically when your ads call for new business despite also using it to get repeat business.

8. Branded Search Trends. How many times did people type the company name in the search box of a search engine and clicked on that site from a listing? This lets a business know the searcher looked for it by name by way of growth marketing/brand marketing initiatives. Couple this with sales trends and get a reasonable composite of correlations to effectiveness.

ROAS (Return on Ad Spend)

9. Cost-to-Benefit Ratio Trends. While sales trends are most important, the second most important metric is how little a business can spend to keep that trend pointing upward, as well as knowing when to increase or level off

spend without slowing the revenue growth pace or losing share.

Before we conclude, I want to park it on cost-to-benefit ratios as a marketing metric to plan and expect. Many times in my career, when I have asked a client decision maker what they want in return for each dollar they spend, they've looked at me like they've never heard of such a thing. The honest ones admit they should know the answer to that, and the best ones barely let me finish the question before stating an extremely ready metric, "I need 4:1 if it is going to be worth my time" or something to that effect.

The reality is that every industry is different. If you combine them all, 4:1 might be the most common. For every dollar they spend, they want $4 back. Trading dollars is a complete waste of energy at 1:1, and 2:1 or 3:1 are good and worthy of patience, but at 4:1 return, the marketing starts producing capital to expand the business or more marketing investment to turn the flywheel even faster.

Before you run away with a metric like 10:1 or 100:1 or some other wishful thinking as to what you tell your vendors you want, remember that there are other influences to the cost-to-benefit ratio. While advertising can amplify a good promise, it can't resurrect a dead or dying business. In fact, it will accelerate the end if you advertise an unkept promise or make one that isn't remarkable. Think about your vendors in these situations. What might you be asking them to overcome? Is your sales team capable of closing the leads your ads find for you? If not, the cost-to-benefit ratio needs to be brought back into reality and perhaps focus your attention on internal improvements to remove the impediments to your advertising. As I promised in the introduction, if you delight customers at every turn, you need less and less of what I am telling you.

Metrics in Perspective

Overlaying the right combination of these metrics will leave a business with very little unknown about the marketing and advertising options used and what to make of the mix. From there, it's just adjusting and fine-tuning as necessary, rather than confusing potential leads with stops and starts or overhauls. Simply put, building a marketing strategy from this perspective takes better care of a future customer's ability to keep a business top of mind and set to buy when the time is right.

Think It Through

* If you are part of the marketing team but not the sales team, how much access do you have to sales trends that you could inspect your work from it?

* Are you familiar enough with your Google Analytics to find and study the trends listed here? How much do you believe knowing these will help you make better decisions?

* Which of all these metrics do you have the biggest chance to improve storytelling? What about making different marketing decisions?

* What is your industry's ROAS ratio? If none exists, what do you think yours should be?

Chapter 15

THE BRAD PITT OF MARKETING

One of my favorite scenes in all sports movie history has to be one between Brad Pitt as Billy Beane and Jonah Hill as Peter Brand in Moneyball. In an off-the-record conversation in a parking garage between Beane and Brand, the reason for the movie emerges. Major League Baseball as an industry has been paying attention to the wrong metrics, and there is a better way of choosing players than paying for typical metrics like homeruns and RBIs. Of course, this assertion by Peter gets Billy interested, because as the GM for the low-budget Oakland A's, he doesn't have enough money on payroll to fetch the big-name players with big bats and hefty salary requirements.

The real-life story of the 2002 Oakland Athletics as told by Michael Lewis in his book by the same name, Moneyball. The movie tells this Cinderella story in such a way that it causes you to see all kinds of applications beyond sports. If in your marketing role, for instance, you feel like "there are rich competitors and there are poor competitors, then there's 50 feet of crap, and then there's you," then you absolutely need to review this mindset evoked by Moneyball, which that line in quotes is a loose interpretation of an admonishment Billy gave when he was trying to help his scouts to prospect differently. They simply weren't going to compete with the typical ways. They were going to have to manufacture wins another way.

To be clear, I'm not asking you to look at all the metrics, I'm asking you to consider the ones you've been looking at might be legacy thought patterns left by an industry that changes out people so much that it doesn't realize the art of wooing of customers disappeared long ago and was replaced by the science of chasing certainty. The main goal has been replaced by side quests that weren't meant to lead. They were meant to add value to reaching the goal. Day after day, headline after headline, the world of local marketing is inundated with the belief that you can save your way to the top. Your limited budgets nod at you in affirmation. But it's the wrong way to look at what's in front of you.

This fact shouldn't discourage you, but rather give you hope, because the most creative minds know a simple truth that restrictions within creative elements act as a catalyst for positive change. Think about it. Would Billy Beane ever have attempted something radical if he were already enjoying the freedom of being at the top? No, he wouldn't. It was the tight limits to their payroll that caused Billy Beane to have to think differently. While one could argue that the A's still haven't won a championship all these years later, their cost per win is always among the lowest in the league, and even better, others have proved him right over and over.

When those teams with better payrolls figured out how to look at on-base percentage as a typically undervalued but extremely important metric, they made better decisions and payroll kept their options diverse. From this, Boston and Chicago ended their decades long droughts of world championships, 86 and 108 years respectively.

You can duplicate this kind of value to your marketing and can keep yours hidden from your competitors a whole lot longer. They'll eventually figure it out, but by then it will be too late. You'll have taken share of the market and delivered a promise they can only hope to copy.

Maybe you aren't under a heavy burden of doing more with less. Maybe you already have a strong budget and have just been trying a little of this and a lot of that. Maybe you've had strong share of the market for years and you feel like it is slipping. All of these stories have a place in the Moneyball of Marketing, and the next chapter is devoted specifically to helping you do that. The way this is done is to stop looking so deeply at our industry's version of homeruns and RBIs, and to look at what gets you on base.

Billy Beane showed his scouts and management team how looking for players who got on base was a better metric to make decisions. If he could get enough of a roster with a high on base percentage for the cost to their payroll, they were going to be an Oakland A. No name player after washed up player were suspect to the rest of the league, but this guy or that guy "gets on base an awful lot for only $285,000." Beane and crew put together a roster of options that weren't trendy or driven by vanity metrics. They got on base, and so can your marketing.

The good news for you is that the alteration of your way to view undervalued metrics in your marketing won't be as public to your competitors as Billy Beane's was for the A's. Both the Red Sox and Cubs have given credit to this way of thinking to manufacture their championships, because it was so publicly obvious it worked. On a small fraction of the budget of the famed Yankees in fact, Oakland pulled out 103 wins on the season and made it as far into the playoffs as the team in pinstripes. And yet, their wins-per-million dollars spent was triple that of the Yankees, 2.51 wins per million dollars spent to 0.82.

If you would like to know what other metrics successful brands study and use to make decisions, read on. But I'll warn you, if you have a bias that can't be questioned like the MLB had for over 100 years, it's going to frustrate you or at least make you want to skip the chapter. But don't do it. A mature mind has the capacity to let two opposing ideas work at the same time without melting down. My hope is that you can study what's next and at least know why you will or won't change.

Think It Through

* What legacy thought patterns of yours have been challenged so far in this book? Do you think you have been in or are now in a place that is ready to consider different metrics?

* Have you found some metrics already in your business that you use that others don't? What kind of impact have you been able to gage from that lesser valued metric?

* If they were going to make a movie about what you are going to pull off for your company like Billy Beane did for his baseball team, who would you want to play you in the movie? Is that the same as who likely would be chosen to play you?

Chapter 16

STEALING TORTURE

P ablo Picasso has been noted to have said, "Good artists copy, great artists steal." Having written hundreds of ads and won my fair share of awards and trophies for helping local businesses get more leads creatively, I can assure you Picasso's words are true. And it isn't just theft of great creatives. It's taking concepts from everything around me that works. To some extent, before I tell you how to build messages that matter to people, you're going to have to realize that everything is in bounds and you have to study everything like it could be something.

Howard Stern once asked Jerry Seinfeld about his process for writing joke material, to which Jerry described what Howard thought was a difficult way to live. Every day, Jerry observes anything and everything and asks himself if this could be something to use later. Every waking moment. When Howard moaned that this sounds like a tortured life, what Seinfeld said next was still somehow funny, in only the way he can be:

"Your blessing in life is finding the torture you're comfortable with ... and you'll do well."

Learning to get comfortable with the tortured life that can find connections with anything for the purpose of better messaging no matter the media is a discomfort you can manage. Figure out what words get people's attention. Watch what triggers people to do things differently. Study what makes people change their minds.

In this chapter, I'm going to give you a few guideposts I've picked up along the way from some really smart people and aggregated them here. None of these are a step-by-step process for building good ads. They are available options to check your work against for refinement. They are ways to train your brain to think differently about the way your customer can be driven to act in a way that is good for you both. Your job is to create enough combinations from these that customers fall in love with you to the exclusion of others.

In full disclosure of who I steal from but not plagiarize when it relates to making good ads, here are the biggest influences on my philosophy and psychology of it all and the work I've studied that you can too:

Roy H. Williams, author of *The Wizard of Ads*.

Why you should steal:

I've arguably lifted the most ideas from him over the years than anyone else. I've hired his people, read all his books, read the Monday Morning Memo, and I go down the rabbit hole. If you know the MMM, you know exactly what I'm talking about. About the only thing I haven't taken advantage of is that I haven't been to Austin while the Wizard Academy is in session. If you pay attention for two decades, you can get a lot from it. But you can probably take the shorter route and enroll in the Academy.

What I got that you can get:

In addition to a monster amount of insight into human psychology and the fun advertising can be, Roy taught me how specificity in your messaging doesn't truly eliminate those outside your specific parameters. "The risk of insult is the price of clarity" is a powerful way thought, but on the other side of the commitment, the clarity doesn't insult non-targets. It gets them to opt in. He has also taught me and thousands of others to focus on feelings and the wallets follow.

Best use case:

If you have trouble seeing the world through your customers' eyes, anything Roy writes will show you how to do it.

Jonah Berger, author of Contagious: Why Things Catch On.

Why you should steal:

Besides this one book, Berger has written others that have similar value, which in this case is both specific ways ideas go viral and real-life case studies that help you understand how it works. The chapters on emotion and storytelling as a means of advancing your business are peppered through the way I even wrote this book. You be the judge as to whether I stole enough of it. There are big time ideas in the book that you could tinker with your own version if you are adventurous.

What I got that you can get:

Stacking possible reasons that ideas spread is a way to solve a lead generation puzzle, and I learned most from this book that most of the reasons people do things or share things are pretty predictable. You'll learn how to tap into so many things from gamifying your offers to making people sound cool when they talk about you.

Best use case:

Your budget is small or you are struggling with sounding like everyone else in your industry, and you need fresh approaches to the conversation to be had with your customers.

Donald Miller, author of *Building a StoryBrand.*

Why you should steal:

So many advertisers get the story wrong, and it makes for devastating results. With a few tweaks to the story, you can spend the same energy and dollars and get better leads and higher volume. Additionally, once you understand the concepts, it translates extremely well between the grand story delivery in mass media to simple conversations with customers via something as anonymous as email.

What I got that you can get:

The story is all wrong if you place your brand as the hero in the customer's story. Too many brands flex their years in business to build trust and spend too much time talking about themselves and place the customer in the place of the "damsel in distress". The customer will buy when you make them the hero of the story in your ads and you are the guide. While it isn't sexy, that story will make you money.

Best use case:

Your company has not been focusing on the customer's problem that needs to be solved and you need help communicating that you can solve it.

Allen Gannett, author of The Creative Curve.

Why you should steal:

There's actually a pattern system you can use to make any idea a creative one, making it accessible to people who aren't necessarily described as creative geniuses. If you can get into enough practice on how it works, good ideas can turn into great ones that sell more of what you offer. Coupled with the familiarity part that Roy Williams teaches, it's a very explosive combination. You will also be encouraged to study literally everything like I have implored you to do here.

What I got that you can get:
What makes ideas creative is that it has one foot firmly planted in the familiar and one foot stepping into the novelty. Too many clever ideas float away because the customer doesn't have it anchored to something they already know or understand. The other half is that only the familiar begins to go unnoticed, so a twist or a novel spin on it is what finishes the creative off and makes it sticky.

Best use case:
Your business needs a fresh approach to something this quite common or regularly ignored by the buying public until it's too far into the process. You might also need a clever way to say the same thing everyone else is saying.

Carmine Gallo, author of The Presentation Secrets of Steve Jobs.

Why you should steal:
No one could state ideas more clearly than Steve Jobs did, and this book explores how someone who wasn't a self-described charismatic person could work with such charisma when he presented. Jobs' relentless devotion to practice gives a clear picture as a marketer how important it is to refine and rehearse for effect all the things you are doing to take good ideas to market and change the way people act as a response.

What I got that you can get:
It's remarkable how much simplicity Jobs used to convey ideas and let the story run the presentation. Focusing on the story

allowed people to feel things that other product launches from other companies couldn't make people feel. Add this to StoryBrand from Miller, and your ability to paint a picture that people will like grows exponentially.

Best use case:
You have a penchant for overcomplicating a good story and need a way to process the simplification without going too far in the other direction.

Additional Worthy Studies.

System 1 – Hinged on the belief that emotion produces feelings and feelings produce action, this group helps marketers tap into which emotions are most effective so you can predict whether your ads are going to work. While monitoring seven basic emotions in the human face, they can see in real time how an ad will grab attention and predict action. Anything you can grab from them is a worthy acquisition.

Magic Numbers – A team of business analysts led by Dr. Grace Kite, these economists study the metrics that matter to determine what's effective and what isn't. While this book covers all kinds of metrics that one might look at once a plan is activated, Kite's team looks even deeper by media. Particularly of interest is her view of what's trendy vs. what's effective.

I should note the honorable mentions are based in the UK, but as I truly believe, human behavior is universally predictable despite market nuances. You can still apply those nuances to your decision-making, but these plus the books I mentioned in this chapter are extremely good at both getting to the root of growth and making it easily digestible. It's fair to say that I skew a little bit on the frustrated side of not getting what I want out of data and insights when it can't be broken down into easily digestible chunks. Everything I discuss in this chapter notably has that. While there are many other entities in the States that have a ton of data, none have been as valuable to me as a marketer as these because of that way I am bent on data consumption. If you like to spend hours in data and can keep from analysis paralysis, I encourage you to look at all kinds of 3rd party data to support your marketing plans.

Think It Through

* What patterns from this list can you detect about the importance of the creative elements to your marketing?

* What other marketing authors and thought leaders would you add to this list? Are there any similarities in philosophy to what is already here?

* What types of conversations are emerging that must be had with your current and future customers? Any media that plays well with this conversation that can help you decide what changes need to be made?

Chapter 17

USING AI TO YOUR ADVANTAGE

D uring the summer of 2025, amid rapid culture shifts in the world, Google made a quiet change to its ecosystem that will likely have lasting effects on how AI is used by small businesses. While this chapter is about what to do with what you have right now, not mentioning these changes would be malpractice. Before I give you tools that will likely change only slightly as time moves on, you need to know what has happened and how that may affect you in the next few years.

You may be surprised to learn that Google's search clicks have taken a hit since Large Language Models (LLM) like OpenAI, Anthropic, and Perplexity have become part of the AI ecosystem.

Even though organic search is projected to also fall, this hasn't happened yet. Google knows what is likely to happen if they don't act, because these LLMs have used Google's search indexed results alongside their own web crawlers to give people a valid answer to their questions within queries. Helping competitive AI with your own indexing capabilities because it is free is a bad position to be in. To combat this shift, not only did Google create Gemini to give specific answers right at the top of the search engine results page above the indexed results, but they also cut off long tail search results. What this means is that they reduced what you and a LLM can see by 90%.

Google has made it harder for competitors' AI tools to access the depth of the answers you will receive from their engine. A deep reservoir of information that used to keep access to information valid and simple is now a shallow pool. This means that visibility of your business will be harder to achieve when your future customers are in the intent stage of their journey to buying. Your first thought here will be to throw up your hands and give up, but the remainder of this chapter will be about tools you can use while the market continues to change.

I will make an additional promise to continue to pay attention to the changes, and when there is another playbook or addendum to this one, I will publish it to my readers to ensure you are using it to the maximum extent possible.

Until then, let's keep this as simple and digestible as possible by first giving you some long-term thinking strategy about AI followed by some short-term tactics you can use right now. You will get out of AI tools what you put in, and the starting point will affect the outcomes you receive. You must be willing to reform that framework if you are going to use it correctly by taking measures to analyze yourself and your cognitive biases as you use it. This way, you don't get output that ruins your plans before you execute. Here are some aspects to consider and pitfalls to avoid in the long-term plan when using AI for marketing.

Using Lazy Visuals

At the time of this writing, video and static visuals still have a long way to go, not just because humans are regularly depicted with inexplicable abnormalities like a 6th finger on one hand, or certain products have pieces notably missing from their design. The possibility for visual greatness using AI is coming, but we need to be extremely cautious until then. Human beings are still quite astute at detecting and more importantly being dismissive of perceived laziness not to be entertained by ads. We want our eyes to be delighted, and many of us have an opposite reaction when we can tell that it's AI-generated. Annoying your customers with lazy ad visuals works against the brand. Be careful not to spend money to hurt your leads in a doubling down on loss.

Consider utilizing a human with an eye for design. Humans who know how to harness AI is better than AI alone, and humans will a wealth of creative capacity are even better than either of these. Be willing to pay for creative elements to be done right, and your marketing will delight your customers.

Too Simple Prompts

The results from your marketing questions might be singular, but the way you get to singular results in AI is back and forth conversation. If you ask one question and want to get one answer, you are likely better off going to a search engine, where you at least get a host of options to choose from. When it comes to AI, context upfront is critical. You can even force it to give you one-word answers, but without nuance, AI will start to veer into the wrong path in its responses. Start with the end in mind in your first sentence in the prompt so you can help the tool know where it is going.

For instance, let's say you are trying to create a strong subject line for an email campaign. If that's all you say in the prompt, your chances of getting something strong and usable are slim. Perhaps instead you can say, "Give me a subject line for an email about our new line of luxury furniture. Using the recommendations of Jeb Blount of Sales Gravy, make the length the most likely to be opened. Following Donald Miller's Story Brand, pose the ultimate question that the opening email will help answer." Even this can go deeper, but ask yourself which prompt will get a better response? Use all you can from your brain to inform the AIs.

Once an end goal is established, you can get off track again if you aren't clear the format and focus of the conversation. Framing things that way will keep you from having to scrap the conversation and start over. If you are looking for a list, say so. If you'd rather have an outline, give that guidance before you put the AI to work. You might find that the answer you get back is relatively short by comparison, but if your prompts are thorough with clear guardrails, it's likely to be much longer but much more validated. In the scenario above, you'd change your prompt to "a list of subject lines" to choose from, and better options might appear.

Stopping Too Early in the Process

Some of the best learnings, ideas, process refinements, and wordsmithing are done just beyond your original query. Before you click away back to what you were working on, ask yourself if there is more you can get from it. Some AI tools do their best to ask you specifically if they can add this or that, but think deeply. By going down the rabbit hole, what else is there to gain if you keep going?

You can use AI to craft a good subject line for a marketing email, and if you keep refining and building, you may come away with a full campaign strategy for the year complete with timing, sequencing, email scripts, and calendar.

Too many users don't build on or revise where they started and the results disappoint. Feel free to come back to the chat later if you want to build at another time. Most AI tools save your chats.

Ignoring Role Play Scenarios

AI tools have a great deal of versatility to be an extra set of eyes or ears in the room, and possibly ANY set of eyes or ears you want. You can have it pretend in the prompt to give you objections, skepticism, drawbacks, and concerns of prospects that your marketing might be able to address. For those who answer to someone above them for approval of their ideas, it's wise to role-play winning that person over too, especially if your talking points are unclear to you.

Perhaps describe your ideal prospect. Give it a script idea for a newsletter, article in a business journal, or some other content repository they would read about you. Ask it to behave like the prospect and tell you what they will like about you or what questions they might have about the material. This will allow you to revise before a prospect ever sees it.

Not Looking at Sourcing

An easy way to use AI incorrectly is to ignore the source that an assertion comes from. Several times, you will be able to follow a source that isn't a source at all, but rather that someone's caption or a blog of some sort used the exact phrasing and AI decided to use it. Especially when facts are involved, you must look at the source of the material you get back. Challenge unsourced information and be skeptical of everything until you can't be. Then you're on to something.

When building and revising with AI tools for your marketing, ask it to share sourcing with each assertion or piece of data in a list, outline, or query result. Click the links associated with it and see if the data says what AI says it does. Think like the prospects and customers you will be talking to. Does the data really say that? What will the customer think about what you are saying? Will they distrust you for using incomplete or misrepresented data?

Expecting AI is Similar

If you have regular access to multiple tools like Copilot, Gemini, Chat GPT, Claude, etc., you will find different levels of value. When it comes to up-to-the-minute intelligence, Gemini is probably your best bet, and Chat GPT is likely the worst. On the other hand, if you are looking for creativity and value of the back-and-forth nature of conversation, none is currently as capable as Chat GPT. All have value, but you must tinker with them each to find out their limitations and use them accordingly with caution.

Think about running the same prompt with each and get a feel for how it responds, whether it can handle the complexity of your needs, and whether up-to-the-minute information is required. Additionally, if you have geographical knowledge that would aid the prompt, you will find that much of the data isn't hyperlocal. See which one sources the best for that, and if it doesn't, figure out which gives you the best expanded market data, national data, or industry data, and go from there.

SEO without GEO

If you have taken great pains to index your website with search engines, as we have discussed in previous chapters, but don't use that same effort to inform AI, you are missing an important future indexing opportunity. Think about it. You have spent years building the keywords and metadata so people using search engines will find you more easily, but what if you could do the same for when they are using AI? Would you want to appear in a sourced result with ChatGPT when someone wants to know more about your product or service? It's early, so you aren't too far behind, but Generative Engine Optimization (GEO) is something your eye should be on for the next few years, as mine will be.

You can make moves right now in some of the following areas:

- Build out customer FAQs on your website.
- Make the answers short and direct.
- Use bullet points as much as possible.
- Customize your content wording without using others' phrasing.
- When you build original content, cite sources so AI will recognize your knowledge associations.
- Put author bios in the content pages to increase authority.
- Consider having a glossary page for terms in your industry.
- If there is a process for what you are promoting, clearly use step-by-step actions in your content.
- Put case studies and industry information into your site.
- If you will use video in your website, provide a transcript to index the text.
- Look at all that is connected to your brand electronically and make sure it's clean and consistent, LinkedIn Posts, YouTube videos, industry articles, etc.

No Policy on Company Information or Breaking Policy

Especially if you are not the owner of the company you are doing marketing for, think twice before uploading sensitive company information. It will surely inform your query results, but it's also free data you're giving to a LLM that is free to use the information you uploaded as it sees fit. If you own your company and you have people supporting your efforts using AI, be extremely protective of how they use your information. The world hasn't seen yet the depth of trouble that will be caused by companies being fast and loose with their data in an AI world. If you get stuck, consider using simulated modules or role-playing like I mentioned earlier. That's not perfect, but it's a much safer position.

Not Arguing With Yourself Enough

We live in a world where people have little capability of considering opposing ideas without melting down in some way. This might be describing yourself if you are honest. If so, you can use AI to test yourself against a confirmation bias and find out you are right; you can also fortify your plans and strategies; or you can completely change course based on it being able to break your bias in a safe space. Let AI tools challenge your suppositions about things, and always dig into the sources with the skepticism level I gave you earlier. If you do that, you will find some obvious bias from AI, but you can work with that if you can detect it.

Whatever you end up doing to maximize it, it's important to underscore that you have no reason to fear it and a lot of reason to be excited. Just like when the internet hit mainstream, there were some growing pains, but as an end user, there's a tremendous upside. While the internet can be a dark and terrible place these days, it can also be a great source of value and connections for little to no cost. Embrace that same value proposition of AI; lean into the difficulty of learning it; you will get out of it more than you put in.

10 Ways to Put AI into Practice Today

In the spirit of practicing what I preach, I asked ChatGPT about what you as a small business can do right away to get useful practice with AI in a way that moves the leads forward. Feel free to use what I told you with more specificity, but here is a great starting point for your next interaction with AI for your business:

10 Everyday AI Habits for Local Business Owners G Marketers

(Lead generation made simpler, smarter, and more consistent)

1. **Write Smarter Responses**

   Use AI to quickly draft professional, friendly replies to leads (texts, emails, DMs). It keeps the response time fast and tone consistent.

2. **Always Have Fresh Social Posts**

   Treat AI like your daily content buddy. Spend 5 minutes a day asking it to draft one post, caption, or idea to keep your business visible.

3. **Test Ads Before Spending**

   Ask AI to generate multiple ad versions (headlines, calls to action) before running a campaign. Pick the best one instead of guessing.

4. **Keep FAQs Ready**

   Load your most common customer questions into AI and use it to generate clear, consistent answers. Great for staff training or social replies.

5. **Polish Your Pitch**

   Whether it's your 30-second intro, voicemail script, or "about us," run it through AI every so often to keep it sharp, simple, and engaging.

6. **Spot Patterns in Leads**

   Feed AI a list of recent leads (even simple notes in Excel) and ask what they have in common — location, timing, service requested — to see trends you might miss.

7. **Turn Reviews Into Marketing**

   Copy-paste a good customer review into AI and ask it to create a social post, testimonial graphic, or even a quick thank-you message template.

8. **Prep for Calls or Meetings**

   Before calling a new lead, ask AI to outline a few conversation starters, objections you might face, and quick ways to build trust.

9. **Sharpen Follow-Up**

   Use AI to brainstorm short, creative follow-up messages so you don't send the same old "just checking in" email that gets ignored.

10. **Keep Learning in Minutes**

    Spend 5 minutes a week asking AI: "What's one new way businesses like mine are using AI for marketing?" That drip of ideas keeps you ahead without overwhelm.

Think it Through

* What ways can you utilize AI better in your prompts and conversation with it?

* What kinds of immediate impact can you make for your website and other online spaces with Generative Engine Optimization?

* What biases do you have about your brand that you can challenge to make your marketing better?

Chapter 18

ABOUT YOUR SALES REPS

I n 1947, the Christmas movie classic Miracle on 34th Street hit theatres worldwide and became an instant success. A quirky man playing Santa Claus for Macy's claimed to be the real Kris Kringle, and what unfolded became legendary. The story is so full of holiday magic and clever characters, it's no wonder the tale has endured. The film won three Academy Awards, and it has been named to many lists of favorites over the years and has even been redone.

One plot twist occurs when good-natured Kris informs frustrated parents where to get certain toys when Macy's is out of stock. He couldn't handle the idea of a child asking for something while sitting on his lap and parents not being able to fulfill the Christmas wish. What started as a point of contention with Macy's management, Mr. Macy himself relished the idea of sending parents to Gimbels due to one hidden fact: "putting public service over profits" was the right thing to do. As Kringle put it, "If we haven't got what a customer wants, we'll send him where he can get it."

Here's my own plot twist to this metaphor: while many of your vendors are diversifying their offers to you, there still isn't any one vendor who can offer you everything you need, no matter how much they insist they do. You'll have to find your Christmas media wish list fulfilled at more than one media store. Furthermore, you'll also have to find yourself a Santa willing to be transparent about what his store can and can't do while also intelligently sending you to the right places to have each box checked in your fledgling lead gen program.

In today's media landscape, this is an extremely tall order, and not likely to be found. But if you are diligent, you can manufacture it by knowing what to look for, how to communicate your desires to each vendor, and like the parents in the movie, reward the effort with billing that brings you leads. The following is a list of things to think about, what to recognize in your media sales reps, both good and bad, and seize the right opportunities when all media appears to be equal to you.

Truth #1: Your sales reps are rarely focused on your actual needs to build leads and build better leads.

The reality is that some can do it well anyway, so this truth shouldn't make you meltdown or shut down. It just means that you will have less outside help from your vendors in looking at what you need without bias. Instead of them looking for what helps you most, they'll find what helps them most and you'll have to be your own hawk, scanning the data and sourcing for whether it also helps you.

Before you give them all two strikes before they enter the batter's box of your office, understand that today's media sales reps are under a significant amount of pressure to deliver for the companies they work for. Most of their leaders have taken big risks in adding more products to their offerings, trained them very little because speed is more important than effectiveness, and expected them to make the new offers profitable. The client's fit for this does not enter the equation many times until it's too late if at all. Because the speed has put them first to market, the immediate successes in their numbers tricks them into thinking they should do it again with more products. While the ones who like to buy the newfangled offers makes it look like a good idea, it makes diligent clients like you frustrated that no one is listening or at least paying attention to how the new products fit into your company's lead generation ecosystem.

Your mission with this truth is to pay close attention to who can concentrate on leads, and like St. Nick, recommend things to you whether they make any money from it or not but do so because it fits the plans they've earned the right to know about. And how do they earn the right to know about them? Well, that brings me to truth #2.

Truth #2: Your sales rep needs to know as much about the purchase funnel or more than you do.

Too many times, vendors may sell multiple options but can't detect what is right or wrong about it even without knowing your plans. For instance, a vendor can have a strong value to offer with their multi-format radio plan and even some online display ads. But what if your website does not drive the leads well? Your radio rep needs to be able to identify this issue and make recommendations to fix that before doing any display ads for sure, let alone the reach value it offers with the radio option. It could make things much worse for how good it is at driving interest.

The potential to drive a lot of leads to a website with issues will not only make leads fall out of the funnel, it will mistakenly have you believe that radio doesn't work and neither does display advertising. So not only will you abandon radio from that one vendor inappropriately, you'll also decline display from everyone else who sells it. And no one spoke up that the real inhibitor was something that only another vendor can fix.

You must find sales reps who ask questions focused on your funnel and make recommendations from your answers whether they drive revenue for their company or not. If you get one of these, hold onto them for dear life, and as they learn more and reveal more in this cause-effect relationship, you will have someone looking on your behalf out there without having to be a paid member of the team. Bring them into every conversation you can and give them the freedom to create. This is a huge value if you can find this. You may never find one, because so few actually understand the whole funnel and their place in it, or the value to balancing media correctly; but if you do, all them in your circle as far as you can.

Truth #3: Your best sales rep options do not have a unique age or gender, but definitely have a unique set of motivations and experiences.

With the reality of the first two truths providing you a reason to be closed-off, this truth is going to have you open up, or at least, get the seller to open up. Get them to tell you about themselves like they are being interviewed for a job, because they are. Center your questions around the answers of which give you a keen understanding about their motivations and experiences outside of media. Here is what you are looking for:

1. Experience with both traditional media and online media – these reps are likely to have a better understanding of the funnel and their place in it.

2. Problem-focused questions – these reps may not know how to solve the problems themselves, but knowing what your problems are, marketing or otherwise, they may get the right internal people involved to help solve them or even better, people outside the company they can refer to who will help you solve them.

3. Experience selling high-ticket items, in or outside media – these reps don't have to be taught to aspire for you very much. In over two decades working with media sales reps, the ones who think too small are those who have never

handled a lot of money and can't fathom your aspirations to grow by $5 million this year let's say. They'll pitch too little and it won't work or they'll see dollar signs and pitch too much without really understanding the gravity of the situation. Rarely is it the latter, but it's happened. But if they have bought or sold six-figure sums, like a house for instance, you can trust them ot handle a bit more financial knowledge.

4. A deep network of contacts in and outside of media – these reps are more likely not just to identify the problems, but also will be able to make solid recommendations on who to pull into the situation for you. If they are involved in the same local networking organizations as you or volunteer for similar organizations in their free time, you can guess their network is better than average. The diversity of experiences is a tremendous help to you even if you don't need it right now.

One could argue that these aspects will only fetch an industry veteran, and that's truly possible, but many veterans of this business have not evolved with consumer behavior but have had their product offerings evolve on them without their adaptation to them. They knew a world that was a simple product that's sold itself, and they, despite being in the business 30 years, are more likely to have 15 two-year experiences cycled over and over than three decades of self-reinvention for clients' sake.

An ignorant upstart with very little to know experience presents you with drawbacks too, but the flip side is that they likely have very few bad habits and likely only know an offering that is deep and diverse. Today's new media sales reps either come from other industries or don't know a world that isn't "digital." Of course, this does not make them better, and their contacts are negligible; but their ability to be molded into what you need of them is high.

Now What?

In either case, industry veteran or ignorant upstart, you'll have to decide on the "would-you-rather" scenario. Both will have to earn your trust with time and focus on your needs. If one of them is reading this right now, I can encourage them that there is a payoff like Mr. Macy promised his sales and marketing teams. They'll have a hard time believing me or even if they do, they'll still have a management team with goals not suggestions. They'll have to balance that. You're going to want to be closed off to either end of this scale if you don't find an experienced rep who is motivated to serve, knows the marketing ecosystem, and has the relational chemistry adaptability to fit your style.

Make them earn it, but trust them when they do. Too many clients and agencies play cat-and-mouse games with reps so they can feel important; they demand things they shouldn't because they don't reward effort; and they make promises they never intend to keep. You should understand that they will have other clients like this and will likely expect the same from you. Be different. Say what you mean and mean what you say. Reward effort and results. Reward those who can do both well. One thing your reps will never say out loud is that when a client is the undesirable kind I mentioned, they will get exactly what they pay for and nothing more. It's the only control over their environment a rep has. On the other hand, all kinds of perks exist for the client who is collaborative, graceful, and aware of how they are perceived. I hesitate even mentioning what some of those are due to variances within each company, but suffice it to say, a rep can make your life easier both in media and in interpersonal scenarios. Very few media buyers understand this to their own detriment.

Think It Through

* What ways do you typically behave with media sales reps? Are you closed off or open to trusting if earned?

* What ways might you need to adapt your style with reps based on what you learned here?

* What questions can you ask to determine whether a rep is ready to learn more? What questions should they be asking you?

Chapter 19

HOW TO BUY STREAMING TELEVISION ADS

've debated all while writing this whether to choose this chapter for inclusion. Streaming TV ad options continue to change rapidly, but it doesn't negate your need to diversify into it. My hope here is that what I can tell you has enough shelf life to be as valid as the rest of this; however, I don't expect it will, so please take what I am telling you as things stand locally in the fall of 2025. Assuming you have alignment with a media sales rep you trust as I articulated in the last chapter, you need to know what your options are and certain rules about them.

Rule #1 – You don't have to buy streaming TV options from one of your TV vendors, but the data and performance are typically going to be better from them.

Everyone is getting into the streaming TV ad offer because direct impressions can be purchased on an exchange on your behalf by your vendors in a scenario much like stocks are traded. Publishers like Prime Video to Pluto TV bundle up impressions and offer them on the exchange where your vendors can buy them for you for a small margin so you don't have to. The bigger you are or the larger the agency you might use, the more likely you can bypass the local vendor and buy from the exchange yourself.

But for most of my readers, a direct client can have a vendor get them. The advantage here is two-fold. If you trust this vendor partner, it's one-stop shopping. You can buy TV from another vendor you trust without having to add another one. And since most of the vendors, especially those in mass media can buy them for you, you can couple the effect of TV driving awareness with the kind of TV that can drive intent through this one person.

The second advantage is that in some cases, especially the cable/broadband providers, there is first-party data on the individual households you will reach that adds more depth to the rich purchasing options. It might be normal to think you want adults between 25 and 54 years old, but what if their first party data can help your used car lot ignore these typical boundaries and perhaps reach households within the geography that also have a certain credit score or are shopping for automobiles with their online behaviors? And since you aren't buying spots but impressions, you have a high likelihood of waste reduction. It's not perfect, but it's really good, which leads me to Rule #2.

Rule #2: Since you are buying impressions closer to your target and not spots, your dependence on brand appeal must be reduced.

Too many of your competitors right now are getting hung up on wanting to be on YouTubeTV or Paramount+. This is a tremendous advantage for you because the simple fact is that in the streaming universe, you are not following a network or platform anymore. You are following an audience. As long as the audience you want is watching, you won't care when they see it or what platform they are seeing it on. Even your vendors are going to fall in line with your competitors most of the time because they still have a hard time understanding it, but you don't fall victim to it. You'll reduce the amount of available options you have and will likely pay more to get it because it is a premium when it doesn't need to be bought as one.

To illustrate this, let me back up twenty years to a time when cable TV was in its heyday. A rep could walk in and say they can get your ad on ESPN or HGTV and people would just buy it because there was a general understanding of the audience's reduction of waste and higher likelihood to be a particular kind of target. There was very little data to show the value of that audience beyond some qualitative data and the groundswell of demand for such networks. But here's the thing, if cable were to be purchased on a

CPM basis, either then or now, people would be buying very differently.

Let's say you want a homeowner who has children and pets. HGTV sounds like a perfect fit. After all, your cable sales rep has plenty of data that shows homeowners watch these shows. To reach 1,000 people, it might cost $85 in its prime and in a primetime spot in the evening when more people are watching TV. But at the same time, those same types of people who fit the demographic are watching Animal Planet during all parts of the day and the cost to reach those 1,000 people is $1.50. Which would you buy? If you are following my point, you absolutely load up on Animal Planet because for cost, the value is enormous comparatively. But to finish my point, too many advertisers opt for the HGTV primetime ads and get a fraction of the value. The sexiness of the brand appeal of such a network raises inventory pressure and therefore forces price increases. All the while, you can drive a truck through Animal Planet and enjoy a ton of value because it isn't sexy.

Streaming is currently dealing with this as a problem. Every option of delivering video ads have relative value, but advertisers chase the brand appeal of a platform and make the value of the audience secondary. If you can zig while the market zags, there is tremendous opportunity for you to beat the market for less. While the wow factor of being on Netflix is cool, a potential $57 CPM cannot compete with the effectiveness of a $37 CPM that is just purchasing your intended target on a one to one basis, and until platforms like Netflix can figure it out, it won't make a lot of sense for local advertisers to want their vendors to get it for them.

Rule #3: What used to be called fragmentation and seen as a bad thing, TV viewership diversification means you can get a more validated audience.

One of the biggest drawbacks in the early days of local cable TV ad sales was that viewership was too fragmented. Stalwart local brands that wanted the power of reach felt like cable couldn't cut it as a TV option. Only part of the market had cable; only part of the audience watched a few networks; and only a few households watched as many as 12-15 networks when there were forty ad-supported channels or more. It just seemed like the cost to reach them seemed too high, like they were having to dig a lot more for a small root when a wide trough dug by broadcast could do the job.

The problem is that cable audiences kept growing and buyers figured out that frequency could add another layer that broadcast's reach for video couldn't match. At some point, about 2004 or so, the combined ad-supported cable reach in any given market was more than that of the combined broadcast reach. And until the housing crisis of 2008, it enjoyed a small golden age. But on the horizon loomed this streaming TV world and when it arrived, it did it all over again.

This time, however, the system was easier to understand audience specifics and reduce waste even further because it was now being purchased on an audience guarantee of sorts rather than just an educated guess about that audience. To add a lot more value, the daily audience of streaming options has dwarfed both cable and broadcast so that nearly half the audience is ad supported streaming. Ad-supported cable and broadcast have to combine entirely to reach more audience than the splintered streaming audience can reach at the time of this writing.

Rule #4: Because not all video impressions are created equal, you must put attention on the kind of video ad impressions you are buying when the CPMs have a wide range of costs.

While this chapter is all about streaming, I have to bring in the other options now so you can see clarity. Below, in each tier of CPM, I'm going to show you what the options are so you can formulate what you might consider when reps come hawking the newest available kind of impressions.

Tier 1 – Low CPMs ($5-$15)

Buy This When:
You buy these impressions when you want a lot of volume during a short period of time to flood the marketplace. Use these as awareness and don't push too hard on targeting.

Available Options:
Instagram/Facebook, TikTok, YouTube Shorts, Snapchat, In-app Video, Place-Based Digital Out of Home (Gas Stations for example).

Tier 2 – Mid Range CPMs ($15-$35)

Buy This When:

You buy these impressions when you want more engagement from the middle of the funnel with something more sustainable to a more specific target. The quality of the environment is better and the scale has more flexible options.

Available Options:

FAST Channels, YouTubeTV, Private Marketplace (that exchange I was referring to), Cinema, Cable TV, Higher-end DOOH (airport terminals for example), Programmatic CTV.

Tier 3 – High CPMs ($35-$70+)

Buy This When:

You buy these impressions when you want surgical-like targeting on a high-conversion tactic. You'll pay more for the validated reach, but the content will be premium on a premium screen, typically.

Available Options:

Broadcast TV (for environment not targeting actually), MVPD addressable (from the cable/broadband provider), CTV direct from the platform (think Hulu, Peacock, etc., not local vendors).

Of course, with all of these, there are outliers. Please don't take these boundaries as brick walls. There are always exceptions on both sides of the boundary with each tier. I mentioned traditional linear cable TV possibly being a dollar or two per thousand. That can happen quite a bit and at the same time if you want Monday

Night Football on traditional ESPN delivery locally, you might pay well over $100 CPM. Furthermore, I mentioned it at the beginning, but over time, much of this may fluctuate widely. I wrote this because you need to be able to start somewhere, so I am drawing a line for you to launch from.

Think It Through

* What kinds of streaming and newly available media have your local reps tried to tell you about that you will no longer systematically ignore?

* Based on your current strategies, which ways can you incorporate the new way of buying media to add value to your plan?

* What are some of the legacy thought patterns you might have that must shift in order for you to stay on the cutting edge of building your leads locally?

CONCLUSION

O n his deathbed in 1543, Nicolaus Copernicus published his life's work, after delaying it for decades. There was so much pressure not to rock the boat, and *On the Revolutions of the Heavenly Spheres* was most certainly going to do that. For most of the centuries before, the world of math, science, and even religion had commonly believed incorrectly that the earth was the center of the solar system. Very few others had ever suggested that the earth revolves around the sun instead of the other way around, but as we know now, they and Copernicus were right.

Copernicus waited decades to publish his work because of his concern for being vilified for trying to change everyone's minds on previously settled science. Doing so at the time of his death meant he wouldn't see much of the persecution that others saw when testing his theory. Kepler, Galileo, and even Newton found heliocentric theory to be fact, but some of them and many others received extremely harsh criticism first by scientists and mathematicians, and lingering negative effects by culture and the Church, both Protestant and Catholic. The first group didn't fully adopt this theory as fact for 150 years and it took nearly 300 for the rest of the world to follow culturally and religiously.

But everything changed for science, math, and technological advancements due to this correction in theory to the sun being the center of our solar system. Besides astronomical changes, physics had a new set of rules, gravity was clearly understood, and the birth of the scientific method gave way to all kinds of study and understanding of our world. Copernicus never got to see the changes, but I would bet he would be prouder of his work than he originally thought he would be.

Now, I'm no Copernicus. The soft way I've brought my theories of media to you isn't waiting until my deathbed, at least I don't think so. And while I think it could change the world for a lot of local marketers, I don't think it will be celebrated for generations like Copernicus' writings have been. But I do share this with him ... I am certain the way I am telling you it works opens up tons of possibilities for thousands of companies to grow their businesses with clarity and confidence from the benefit of a better, fresher perspective. I do expect some to come at me with new information or rebuttals, but I'm here for it. No one gets burned at the stake for being contrarian in media like they did when they suggested mankind is not the center of the universe.

I'm ready to keep the conversation going and welcome the grind to get you leads. If you'd like to continue on your own, with a format for building your new strategy yourself, visit www.leadorbleedbook.com, and I'll send you a free toolkit to do this for yourself in a step-by-step process that you can customize for your unique situation. Otherwise, find me on LinkedIn, and let's talk about your leads.

ACKNOWLEDGEMENTS

I'd be nowhere without Jesus, so my gratitude must extend to Him first. Anything good you see me do or any wisdom I have to share is because He gave it to me. I am grateful for this, whether or not I've sold a single copy of this book, and what I can tell you about Him is worth more than anything else these pages give you.

When my kids were growing up, I was hopeful one of them would get into the creative/advertising/marketing business like me. I've been blessed to have all four of my grown children doing something in the industry now. I have my wife Alica to thank as well for putting up with endless conversations about logo color schemes, character designs, font styles, and memory hooks. She really has had to deal with a lot from all of us, and family dinners just went differently than she probably would have wanted a lot of the time.

But I want to thank my daughter Jill, especially for leaning directly into the concepts I shared in this book and teaching me how far I can take it. The value of her willingness to keep me on the pulse of the industry can't be overstated. I taught her, but now she teaches me, and she's made this book better for you because of it.

As a newly minted sales manager in 2006, I met Jim Doyle. He saw something in me that few could see, sometimes even before I could see it. I'll never be able to give him back what he's given me in wisdom and insights, and he knew that when he was doing it.

Finally, I want to acknowledge Jeff Gregg and Bill Chambers, who, for large portions of my career and at different times, have let me tinker with my assertions on the industry in a corporate environment that wasn't immediately looking for start-up energy tucked in a mature business model. I can't thank them enough for running cover and trusting that I'd come through with value to make it worth it.